AWESOME
Art Activities
for Kids

AWESOME ART ACTIVITIES for Kids

20 **STEAM**
PROJECTS TO SPARK CREATIVITY
AND IMAGINATION

LUCY SONG

ROCKRIDGE
PRESS

For general information on our other products and services or to obtain technical support, please contact our Customer Care Department within the United States at (866) 744-2665, or outside the United States at (510) 253-0500.

Rockridge Press publishes its books in a variety of electronic and print formats. Some content that appears in print may not be available in electronic books, and vice versa.

TRADEMARKS: Rockridge Press and the Rockridge Press logo are trademarks or registered trademarks of Callisto Media Inc. and/or its affiliates, in the United States and other countries, and may not be used without written permission. All other trademarks are the property of their respective owners. Rockridge Press is not associated with any product or vendor mentioned in this book.

Series Designer: Katy Brown
Interior and Cover Designer: Tricia Jang
Art Producer: Melissa Malinowsky
Editor: Eliza Kirby
Production Editor: Emily Sheehan
Production Manager: Holly Haydash

Photography © 2022 Lucy Song; Shutterstock, p. ii; iStock, pp. vi; x, 14, 100; All illustrations used under license from Shutterstock.com

Paperback ISBN: 978-1-63807-129-7
eBook ISBN: 978-1-63807-526-4
R0

For all the children
who want to be an artist
and more.

CONTENTS

INTRODUCTION

Hello, friend! I'm so happy you've picked up this book to join me in a creative adventure through the world of visual art. Together, we'll learn what art is, how artists think and make, and how art connects to science, technology, engineering, and math (STEM). Along the way, you'll also discover more about yourself, how to express what you've learned, and how to not only love your **masterpieces** but also enjoy the process. You'll be welcoming that waste bin of crumpled-up "mistakes" in no time. You'll learn by doing with the twenty fun, creative, and inspiring art projects in this book.

Back up. Art and STEM? How does that work? Gone are the days when grown-ups might tell you to choose one or that you're too artsy for math. You, my friend, can do more!

How do I know? My name is Lucy Song. When I was growing up, I felt stuck in the middle. I loved technology, and I loved art.

At night, I would code a new personal website nearly every week. By day, I took extra art classes to learn how to sketch, draw, and shade. I hadn't known there was a world that combined my passions until I became a grown-up and saw technology and art working together. I've worked as a graphic designer, a prop technician, and a stylist and worked my way up to becoming a creative director—a person who leads a team of photographers, designers, stylists, makeup artists, and more. Today, I've dedicated my career to helping young people know and love the possibilities of art and STEM.

Okay, let's stop calling it art and STEM, shall we? When you add art to STEM, you get . . . STEAM! So, you see, this is not your average arts and crafts book. It's about inspiring you to make art and to learn STEAM. In the projects, you'll sew e-textiles, wrap things like a cocoon, and sculpt like a 3D printer. From time to time, you might

come across some words you might not understand. When this happens, just flip to the glossary, beginning on page 105. This is where you'll also learn more about STEAM.

In these twenty amazingly fun projects, you'll get easy-to-follow, step-by-step photos for you and a grown-up to do at home. Most of the materials and supplies you'll need are right around you. If you don't have some things, that's okay. The projects will list other suggestions, but remember to use your imagination, too, because you can even paint with yellow mustard!

My hope is that you'll end up with a room full of wonderful conversation-starting artwork that you can hang on the wall, gift to a friend, or share with your class. Now let's send you off on a journey of creativity, new ideas, self-discovery, and STEAM explorations.

Are you ready? Turn the page to begin your adventure!

Part I

THINK LIKE AN ARTIST

Have you ever wondered what art is? Can you think of a time when you picked up a paintbrush, opened some playdough, or popped the lid off a marker to make art? How did you decide what to make with it? Can a monkey wearing a hat made of playdough be art? Have you ever asked yourself, "Hmmm, what color should I use?" Yes? Then it's safe to say you already think like an artist.

Artists love to ask questions. Does this sound familiar to how you might begin projects in ⓢⓣⓔⓐⓜ? You bet it does! Artists start with a question, and when they think deeply about it, they call these thoughts their **musings**. Musings are then doodled or written down in a sketchbook. A sketchbook is a magical place. It's a place where no one will judge your ideas, you don't have to follow the rules, and you can be playful, follow your curiosities, and spark new ways of doing things. The sketchbook is where your inspirations are born. So keep one at your side as we begin your creative journey!

Chapter 1

WHAT IS ART, ANYWAY?

Paintings on the walls, sculptures on pedestals, sketches of yourself, a baby bottle wrapped in threads, and a robot-made drawing. These are examples of visual art you will make from this book!

This chapter will talk about what art is, how artists think and make, where we see art in the world, the impact it makes, and how important art is to STEM. Most importantly, we'll learn how you are already an artist and how you can start making your own masterpieces.

WHAT IS ART, AND WHO'S AN ARTIST?

How do we sort between what is art and not art? This question has been debated for centuries. One of the oldest drawings found is a cave painting in Indonesia, and it tells the story of one warty pig watching a possible fight. Today, we still use drawings to help us tell stories. Does that mean all art needs to tell a story?

Some may say yes, but art was once about talent, too. In the fourteenth century, during the **Renaissance art** period, artists could only sell their artwork if they were members of a guild. The only way to join a guild was to create a valuable masterpiece, an artwork that displayed the artist's greatest talent and skill. At this time, value was based on how realistic and beautiful the art was. Then in the early 1800s, the camera was invented, and realistic art became less valuable over the wonder of photographs. By the mid-1800s, a wave of artists started to create **modern art**, representing the world and emotions through symbols, shapes, colors, and texture. Art became valued for its originality and how intelligent the meaning behind the art was—which partly still holds true today.

Modern artists mused over the question, What is art? Then they challenged it. **Dada** artists began to take objects they found, such as an old bicycle wheel, and display them in art galleries as a statement. Dada artists believed anything an artist labels as art is art. Many people were confused because the objects were not beautiful, it didn't take talent to find an object, and there was no clear story. It was also not unique because the same bike wheel could be found all over the city.

Today, we understand that art can be anything, but art is not everything. We're back to the question we started with: How do we sort between what is art and not art? It's up to the artist to decide.

Then who can be an artist? There are varying opinions on who can and cannot be an artist. However, many grown-ups would agree with **cubist** painter Pablo Picasso that "every child is an artist."

HOW DO ARTISTS CREATE?

Take a stroll through an art gallery, and you'll see all the ways an artist creates. As you walk from room to room, you might see paint on canvas, collage on paper, big shapes made from stone or clay, and screen-printed fabrics. These are some traditional mediums in art. **Mediums** are the materials or tools artists use to make their art. Less "traditional" mediums can be computers, film, lights, bricks, plastic bottles, and straws. Do you see a trend here? Yes! You can also use all these mediums in STEM!

The possibilities are endless, so how does an artist choose? Well, it could be a meaningful choice. Maybe chalk reminds the artist of the first medium they've ever held. It could be a practical choice like spray paint for a **mural** on the side of a building because it is quick to use and stands up against the rain. Sometimes the choice can simply be because the artist enjoys it the most.

After an artist has chosen a medium, they will explore and practice different ways to use it. These are what artists call **techniques**. For example, with a crayon, you can draw the outline of a sun and color it in. But did you know you can melt the crayon, smudge it, and scratch into it, too? An artist can use one technique in their art, or they can do more. You don't have to stop there. An artist can also choose to use many different mediums with many different techniques to create one piece of art. This is called **mixed media** art.

Too many mediums and techniques to choose from? That's okay. When we're ready to begin the projects, we'll explore many of these possibilities one at a time. I can't wait! Can you?

HOW DOES ART IMPACT THE WORLD?

Now that we've learned what art is and how an artist thinks and makes it, we can ask ourselves, Why share our art? Does art impact the world? How?

Let's start with an art we all know and enjoy: cartoons! Have you ever wondered how your favorite show came to be? It began with a discovery by a photographer named Eadweard Muybridge in 1878 when he took twelve photos of a horse galloping. After several experiments, tinkering, and the help of some friends, he made those photos "move" to create the first **stop-motion picture**. Today, Muybridge's famous works sit inside the Kingston Museum in London, England. Even though the first-ever stop-motion picture sits inside a museum, we see this art medium everywhere—on TV, in theaters, and in hilarious GIFs online!

Art doesn't just exist in museums. In cities, we see sky-high buildings made by architects. On the streets, we see graffiti made by artists. In shopping centers, we see moving toy displays made by **visual merchandisers** (people who decorate a store). In the classroom, we see students who fashionably style their outfits to express who they are. Every day, art is all around us.

No two people will experience an artist's work the same way. Often, we won't experience art the way the artist thought we would. We all bring our own stories to someone else's, and we'll make our own meanings from it. Art reflects and expresses who we are and how we see the world. This is the beauty of art, and all art is beautiful.

Take a minute to experience the world around you. Can you see all the art you enjoy? Do you feel all the wonders of where art meets STEM?

WHAT'S THE DEAL WITH ART AND STEAM?

Look up across the walls of your bedroom. Do you see books neatly lined up on your shelves or on the floor piled near your bed? Did you know those books were made possible because of STEAM? How, you ask? First, the paper is changed from wood into paper with chemicals concocted by scientists. The paper is then rolled and cut from machines designed by engineers. Writers and illustrators then write and draw their stories. With technology, digital printers are used to fill the pages with ink. Lastly, math is used to calculate the cost of the book for people to buy. Whew! Now that's teamwork. What would happen if one team went missing? Imagine art had disappeared; you'd end up with a book without a story! In this example of making a book, it's easy to see how all the elements of STEAM fit together.

There are other parts of STEAM that also connect but aren't as easy to see. These invisible parts of STEAM are the bigger lessons. In science, we can learn to uncover truths, like why sea levels are rising or how the Earth orbits the sun. In technology, we can learn to believe in doing things we thought were impossible, like talking to someone in another country or skyrocketing to Mars. From engineers, we can learn how to juggle moving parts to make sure everything works well together. In art, we can better understand the way we think and feel and use our musings to inspire creativity or show a new point of view. Lastly, from math, we can learn to think logically and make decisions. Each part of STEAM has something to teach us, and when you learn to apply them together, you can open a world of new ideas to invent, design, solve problems, and make art.

Imagine you had five pairs of goggles, one for each STEAM field. You pick up one pair, and it's an X-ray lens to see how a scientist sees and thinks. You pick up the math pair, and you see the world in numbers, shapes, and grids. Now think about what the world would look like if you piled on all five pairs. Imagine that view. Very few see this way. Why? For a long time, grown-ups thought it was best to teach STEAM as separate parts at separate times. This is changing. Grown-ups are learning to help kids like you to wear all five pairs of goggles by bringing them together. Today, more and more kids are learning to see the world through STEAM.

In this book, you'll learn by doing the projects. Some of these projects will ask you to wear two or three pairs of goggles. In others, you may even wear all five! As you practice seeing the world through STEAM, you'll get closer and closer to making masterpieces unlike anything the world has seen before.

WHAT DO I NEED TO KNOW TO MAKE ART?

The steps an artist takes to get from a blank canvas to a finished artwork is called the **creative process**. One popular process you may want to try is the engineers' process for design. The steps are to ask, imagine, plan, create, and improve. Here is a closer look at what to do at each step.

ASK

What do you wonder about? Doodle or write your question, make a list, or ask a friend the question. Try asking questions about the question. Research some answers and wonder what is missing from the answers you find.

IMAGINE

What do your musings show you? Do they have a color or a texture? What emotions do you feel? Do they remind you of a place or a memory? Doodle, sketch, and write down your thoughts. Use your musings to choose your medium and technique.

PLAN

Think through the steps you would take to make the artwork. What materials and supplies are you missing? When are you and a grown-up available to gather them? When do you have time to begin making art?

CREATE

Take three slow and deep breaths. Notice the light, smells, sounds, and textures in the present moment. When you feel ready, begin. The process is just as important as the final piece. In some art, the process is, in fact, more important! Let go of perfection. You can always return to your art when you feel more ready.

IMPROVE

Choose to start again or share your work with those you love. Listen to what they say and ask questions about what they think. Make notes about how you might be able to make your work better or more challenging.

These steps can guide you, but don't be afraid to create your own process if it doesn't work. Everyone has their own way of doing things. It's important to accept both your own artwork and the artwork of others.

It's okay to not always love the outcome. Having a trash bin beside you is a good sign that you are an artist. It means you're ready to make mistakes and try again.

With the projects in this book, you will learn by doing. With trying anything new, like riding a bicycle, we sometimes fall. Each fall only means you're getting closer to becoming better. If you go in with this mindset, you'll see each time you repeat a project that you're growing closer to what your heart and mind imagined.

Chapter 2

HOW TO USE THIS BOOK

Pixel art emojis, robot-made doodles, and glowing crowns to wear to rule your kingdom are some of the fun art projects you'll work on. You'll learn to create art with rhythm, go with the flow of mistakes, and laugh a little with an animated cookie. These twenty projects will have you exploring new ways of doing things that will surprise you. Along the way, you'll start to pick up how each piece of art is connected to STEM and how STEAM can be part of your path to making inspiring artwork. Get ready to decorate your walls, share ideas with friends, and let your imagination loose!

GETTING READY

Here's what you need to know to get started. Flip through, and you'll see projects that may interest you right away or ones you feel are easy enough to do on your own. As you look further to the back of the book, the projects will get more challenging. You might want to save some of those for when you have a grown-up by your side to help you along. Each project has an estimated length of time to complete; you can use it to ask your grown-up how much time to set aside for you.

Projects are labeled easy, medium, and challenging. Choosing them in that order may work best. Whichever project you choose, always begin with a grown-up reading the introduction to the project and materials list with you. Why? Well . . . art is messy. It's best to be prepared for the mess in a way that a grown-up would say is okay. This will ensure you have fun instead of worrying about the mess you made.

One idea would be to wear an apron and make the art outside on a nice, not-so-windy day. Another idea is to lay down some newspaper or a washable painter's drop cloth to protect the table and floors of your home. A garage with a heater might also be a good art-making space for the winter months. When you can, try to choose a space in your home by a window for natural light.

Once you have your art space set up, read through the materials list and make a list of what you are missing. You can either go out to a local craft store to purchase or look in your home for a substitute. After a grown-up has read the first part of the project with you, be sure to talk about the "Caution" notes together. Your grown-up may choose to do some of these steps for you, or they may stay close by your side to watch.

If you've done all this, you'll be happy to know you've already set yourself up for success.

DOING THE PROJECTS

You might find it easier to follow along with just the pictures at first, but it's best to read the step-by-step instructions as well. Remember, if there are any words highlighted in bold text that you don't quite understand, the glossary at the back of the book will explain the meaning. Be sure to read the "Fun Fact" and "STEAM Connection" sections as well. In these sections, you'll learn more about how the art project is connected to historical inventions and real-world artists and artworks. You'll also uncover STEM explanations to what is happening in your art-making process.

At the end of each project, you'll notice a section that says "Now Try This!" for more ways to do the project. Give them a try to learn new techniques or mediums to use.

ESSENTIAL SUPPLIES

In your home, there are many possibilities to choose as your medium. Here, though, is a list of items you may find yourself reaching for again and again. You may want to gather these essential bits in a small box and label them "art stuff" to make them easy to find.

It's also a good idea to start collecting some used recyclables. You can use a cardboard box to store them until you're ready to use them. Be sure to clean any plastic or Styrofoam before placing it in the box.

TOOLS

- Pencil
- Eraser
- Ruler
- Paintbrushes
- Paint palette (or use an ice cube tray)
- Safety scissors
- White school glue
- Glue stick
- Washi tape (or masking tape)
- Clear tape
- Jar of loose parts (googly eyes, pom-poms, buttons, bottle lids, cotton swabs, etc.)

FOR SETUP

- Artist apron, or an old oversize T-shirt
- Washable painter's drop cloth, or an old bedsheet
- Disposable table cover
- Washcloth or paper towel
- Cup of water to wash brushes
- Natural light from a window

USED RECYCLABLES

- Cardboard boxes
- Newspaper
- Tissue boxes
- Toilet paper roll tubes
- Used Styrofoam trays
- Outgrown clothing
- Plastic bags
- Scrap yarn

Part II

THE PROJECTS

Let's bring the artist out in you. Are you ready to smear paint, tear newspapers, and doodle with glue? The twenty projects in this book will let you explore watercolors, crayons, recycled plastic, string, and cardboard in ways you haven't done before. You'll learn to love the process and express yourself and your ideas through shapes, colors, and symbols. You'll also learn to look at the world like an artist! That's not all. Want to know the best part? When you're done, you'll have a room decorated with artwork you'll love to talk about. Get ready to melt some crayons, slap on sticky notes, and stamp up posters! Flip the page to begin your next masterpiece!

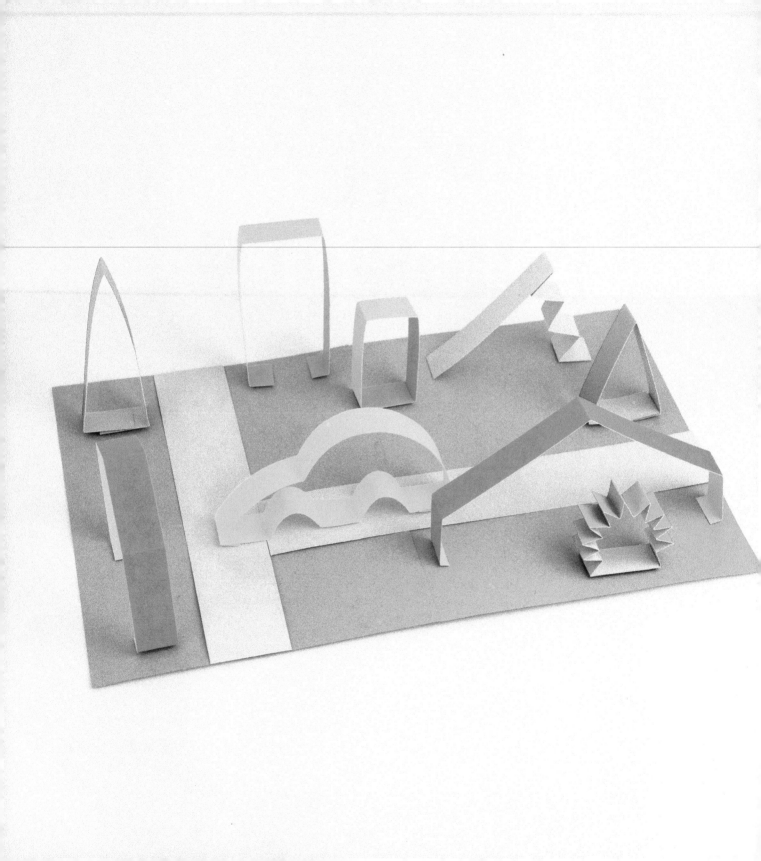

SCULPT A MAP

TIME: 40 MINUTES
DIFFICULTY LEVEL: EASY
MEDIUM: CUT PAPER AND GLUE
TECHNIQUE: FOLDED PAPER SCULPTURE, LINE AND SHAPE OBSERVATION

MATERIALS

- Sketchpad
- Pencil
- Colored cardstock or construction paper
- Clear tape
- Ruler
- Safety scissors
- Glue stick

Let's explore where you're from with a map! Do you live in a city or the suburbs? What kind of lines do you see in your neighborhood? Are there tall rectangular buildings, a triangular slide in a playground, or a rounded bush in the yard? Try outlining the shapes in your mind to get ready to sculpt with paper!

THE STEPS

1. Take a stroll around your neighborhood and make sketches for your map. Find landmarks and ask yourself, "What basic shape can I turn this into?" For example, turn an apartment building into a rectangle or an evergreen tree into a triangle.

2. Tape together two sheets of paper to use as your map base and set them aside.

CONTINUED

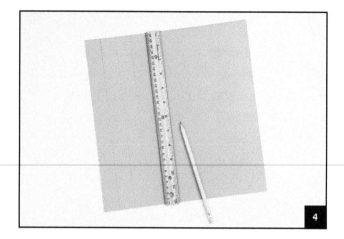

3. Choose four to seven colors for the shapes you'll fold for your map.

4. Draw lines across each sheet with a pencil. Each line should be about 1 inch apart, or the thickness of your ruler.

5. Cut along the lines you've marked with scissors.

6. Fold the strips of paper into shapes from your sketch. Try to keep your shapes as simple as possible. Add an extra fold at each end of the strip to glue it down to the map.

7. Glue each shape to the map base.

8. Share your art with friends and see how similar or different the maps are.

FUN FACT: The largest paper sculpture used nearly 6,000 rolled and connected sheets to create a pyramid-shaped structure.

STEAM CONNECTION: Have you ever wondered who designed your neighborhood? They're a group of people called urban planners and civil engineers. They work to make sure your school, roads, and home are a good community to live in. They use math to calculate how big your school needs to be, how many parks or playgrounds can be added, and how many roads can lead you there.

NOW TRY THIS!

➲ Go beyond your neighborhood and make a map of your favorite places in the world!

➲ Design an imagined world for your dolls and action figures to play in.

PLAY WITH PATTERNS

TIME: 45 MINUTES

DIFFICULTY LEVEL: EASY

MEDIUM: WATERCOLOR
AND WAX CRAYON
ON PAPER

TECHNIQUE: WAX
RESIST WATERCOLOR,
PATTERN AND TEXTURE
OBSERVATION,
DRAWING WITH
GEOMETRIC SHAPES

MATERIALS

- 3 or 4 animal pattern inspirations from toys, stuffed animals, or books
- 3 or 4 sheets of Bristol board paper or mixed media paper pad
- White wax crayon or oil pastel
- Watercolor palette
- Cup of water
- Flat paintbrushes
- Pencil
- Found objects, such as lids, cups, containers, etc.
- Safety scissors
- Washi tape or masking tape

What if a bunny had spots like a cheetah or a bear had stripes like a zebra? In art, we don't always have to follow the rules. Sometimes just having fun is what makes art. This is called **process art**, or making art for the fun of it. In this project, we'll reveal secret animal patterns with a wax crayon and watercolor paints.

THE STEPS

1. Use the animal patterns you found as inspiration and draw a pattern on the paper with a white wax crayon. Be sure to press hard! Repeat this step with the other sheets until you have three or four sheets with a different pattern on each.

2. Paint the entire sheet with one color of watercolor to make your pattern appear! Repeat this step using a different color for each sheet. Set aside and let dry for 15 minutes.

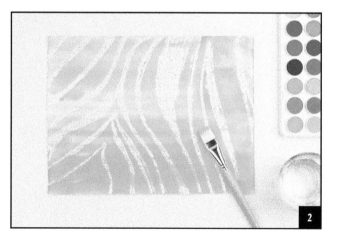

AWESOME ART ACTIVITIES FOR KIDS

3. While you wait, search your home for different shapes to trace. You could use cups, lids, containers, caps, or bottles. Try to look for different sizes of circles, ovals, squares, triangles, and rectangles.

4. When the watercolor is dry, turn the paper over so the blank side is facing up. Trace the shapes with a pencil to create animals, like a bear, a bunny, or an elephant.

5. Cut along the outside lines with scissors.

6. Flip over your art and see what silly animal you've made! If your artwork is curled, lay it flat on a table and pile some books on top. Check back the next day, and it will be ready to tape to your walls!

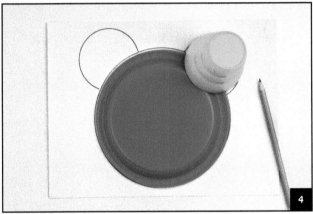

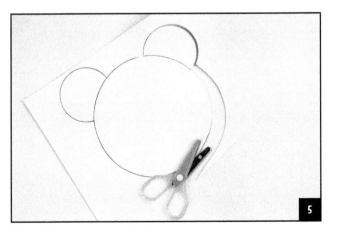

CONTINUED

FUN FACT: Why do zebras have stripes? For thermoregulation! In other words, the black stripes attract light to keep zebras warm, and white reflects light to keep them cool.

●①⑤①◎ CONNECTION: Chemists sort molecules as polar and nonpolar. Water is a polar molecule, and it mixes well with other polar molecules, like watercolors. Wax is a nonpolar molecule and doesn't mix with polar molecules. The wax crayon shows through when you paint over it because nonpolar molecules resist polar molecules.

NOW TRY THIS!

➔ Cut two holes for eyes, then add an ice pop stick to the bottom, and you've got a mask for pretend play.

➔ Explore watercolors with other nonpolar molecules, like oil pastel or even butter!

➔ Look in your closet for more pattern inspirations.

PAINT YOUR THOUGHTS

TIME: 45 MINUTES

DIFFICULTY LEVEL: EASY

MEDIUM: ACRYLIC ON MIRROR

TECHNIQUE: SYMBOLISM

MATERIALS

- Washi tape or masking tape
- Disposable sandwich bag
- Pencil
- Cup
- Safety scissors
- Hand mirror
- Acrylic paint
- Paint palette or ice cube tray
- Paintbrushes
- Cup of water

A mirror reflects an image of you and the world around you. What if you could share a world of your thoughts with someone else? Our thoughts can be ideas that pop up, like a rainbow and a dinosaur. These can become symbols representing an idea, like the sun can symbolize a fun day of play. Would you like to share your thoughts about a fun day? Let's get started with a mirror painting!

> ! **CAUTION:** Acrylic paint will stain. Be sure to protect your art space and wear an apron.

THE STEPS

1. Tape strips of washi tape to a sandwich bag to make a square about half the size of your hand mirror. Make sure each strip is slightly overlapping the previous strip.

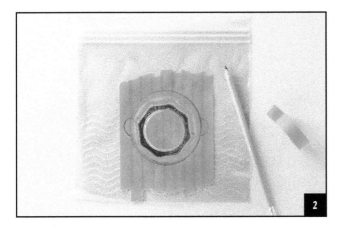

2. Trace a circle using a cup. Add ears to your drawing.

3. Cut out the shape.

4. Carefully peel off the tape from the plastic bag as a single piece and apply it to the center of your hand mirror.

5. Paint a background color on the mirror and let the paint dry for 10 to 20 minutes.

6. Paint your thoughts. Think of symbols you see in your mind. Let the paint dry for 30 minutes.

7. Peel off the tape and share your artwork with a friend. Let them look in the mirror to see their face in your world of thoughts.

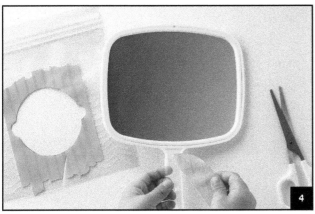

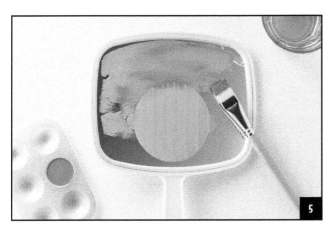

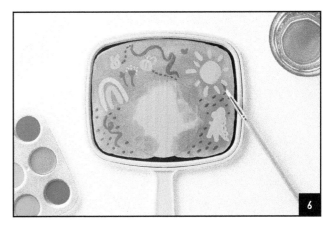

CONTINUED

FUN FACT: World-famous artists like Yayoi Kusama and Michelangelo Pistoletto use mirrors to create their art!

STEAM CONNECTION: How do mirrors work? Humans can only see light. If you're standing in a room with no light, you can't see. Now imagine a large light beam pointing toward you. It bounces off you, shoots toward the mirror, and then bounces back toward your eyes. In physics, we know light can be absorbed, bounced (reflected), or passed through an object. A mirror reflects up to 95 percent of the light shined on it. Because of its supersmooth surface, when the light shines off it and into our eyes, we can see our reflection in the mirror.

NOW TRY THIS!

➲ What happens if you use two mirrors facing each other? Play with mirror and light to inspire your next masterpiece!

➲ What signs and symbols do you see in the world? What hidden meanings do they have? Doodle signs and symbols into your sketchbook as you see them and write notes about what they could mean.

MAKE WITH FOUND OBJECTS

TIME: 30 MINUTES

DIFFICULTY LEVEL: EASY

MEDIUM: FOUND OBJECTS AND FIBERS

TECHNIQUE: FOUND ART

MATERIALS

- Outgrown clothing, such as mittens, socks, shirts, etc.
- Scissors
- Outgrown found objects, such as baby bottles, Velcro shoes, sippy cups, etc.
- Clear tape (optional)
- Newly found object (optional)
- Paper (optional)

How magical is it that a little caterpillar can transform into a butterfly? What if we created an artwork with a symbolic **metaphor** for change and new beginnings inspired by cocoons? In this project, we'll use **found objects** we've outgrown, like a baby bottle, and spin our own cocoon to create a metaphor for change!

CAUTION: Sharp scissors may be needed to cut the outgrown clothing. An adult will need to complete step 1. Remember to ask for an adult's permission to use outgrown objects. You wouldn't want to use an important keepsake!

THE STEPS

1. Cut strips of the outgrown clothing to create ribbons.

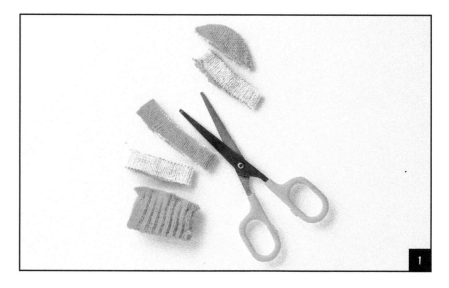

AWESOME ART ACTIVITIES FOR KIDS

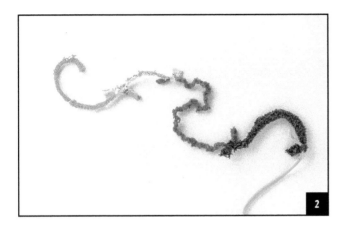

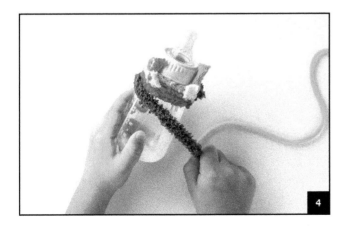

2. Tie together several ribbons with a double knot. Stretch and pull the tied material to make it look like string.

3. Tie the knotted string around your found object to keep it in place or use tape.

4. Spin the ribbon around the object until it's covered and tie a knot at the end when you're done.

5. Optional: Find an object you now use that replaced the one you've wrapped. If you chose a baby bottle, perhaps you now use a cup. Or maybe you used to wear shoes with Velcro, and now you wear shoes with laces. Place this object next to your cocoon. Think about the change you've been through. Do you feel you've grown wings like a butterfly? Add some wings with paper and tape or with the leftover fabric. Take photos of them side by side and share your artwork!

CONTINUED

FUN FACT: This project was inspired by Judith Scott, a famous artist known for her cocoon-like textile sculptures. You can see her work at the Museum of Modern Art (MoMA).

S T E A M CONNECTION: **Maria Sibylla Merian was a pioneer in the discovery of metamorphosis with her scientific illustrations. In biology, metamorphosis describes any animal that goes through a big physical change, like the transformation of a caterpillar to a butterfly. Other animals that go through metamorphosis are frogs, jellyfish, and grasshoppers.**

NOW TRY THIS!

- Some animals shed skin as they grow, like a crab or a snake. What found objects could you use to create a metaphor of outgrown skin?
- Found objects can become something new by painting them a new color or decorating them. What else can you transform?

CUT AND PASTE A MESSAGE

TIME: 30 MINUTES

DIFFICULTY LEVEL: EASY

MEDIUM: CUT-AND-PASTED PAPER AND PRINTED PAPER ON PAPER

TECHNIQUE: PHOTOMONTAGE, COLLAGE

MATERIALS

- Newspapers, magazines, printed images, or photocopies
- Safety scissors
- Colored cardstock or construction paper
- Glue stick

Someone once said, "A picture is worth a thousand words." In this project, we'll explore how to create visual messages with found images using a technique called **photomontage**. Get ready to flip, snip, and paste!

THE STEPS

1. Flip through a magazine or newspaper and tear or cut out pictures that inspire you or spark an idea about a message you would like to say with your art. In this example, a child in a cape sparked a "saving the world" theme. The ducks and chemical vials inspired the idea of saving the ducks from pollution.

Helpful Tip: If you don't have magazines or newspapers to cut up, check your local library for images and photocopy them. Remember to bring coins for the copier.

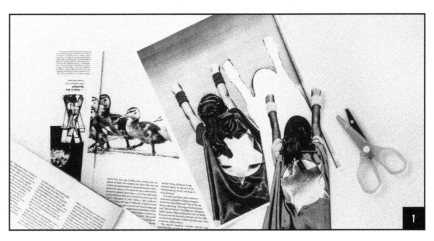

CONTINUED

2. Cut up some colored paper to fill and add textures or symbols to express your message clearly. In this example, a little research led to the idea of how ducks can be saved from the chemical pesticides in our lawns. Blades of grass are symbolized with cut green paper and a river of chemicals with cut gray paper.

3. Glue the cut photographs and paper in a way that will help the message be understood.

4. Share your artwork with friends and family and see if your message can be read.

4

STEAM CONNECTION: With computer technology, artists today can create photomontages with digital software. Among the first to play with Adobe Photoshop was Maggie Taylor. The software became so popular that people now use the term *photoshopped* for digitally montaged photos.

NOW TRY THIS!

- After listening to some feedback about your art, add or take away parts of your photomontage that might help make your message clearer.

- Use watercolors, markers, or crayons to draw on top of your photomontage to add more meaning. Yellow can add a message of happiness or warmth. Red can add a message of love or anger.

PRINT A POSTER

TIME: 30 MINUTES
DIFFICULTY LEVEL: EASY
MEDIUM: ACRYLIC PAINT ON PAPER
TECHNIQUE: RELIEF PRINTMAKING

MATERIALS

- Used Styrofoam food containers, cleaned
- Safety scissors
- Tracing paper or parchment paper
- Pencil
- Acrylic paint, tempera paint, or water-based block-printing ink
- Plastic plate or cookie tray
- Sponge roller or rubber brayer
- Cardstock or poster paper
- Washi tape or masking tape

Would you like to be class president one day? Or maybe host a party or a bake sale or sell lemonade? There are so many wonderful reasons you might need to make dozens of posters. Posters are works of art, too! We'll explore **printmaking** to create posters for your next event in this project.

 CAUTION: Paints are not washable. Be sure to protect your art space and wear an apron.

THE STEPS

1. Cut the Styrofoam to make a flat sheet for easy stamping, removing any curved edges or sides.

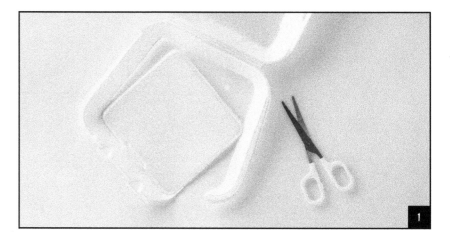

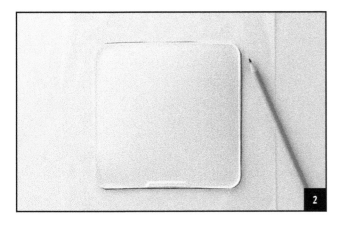

2. Trace your flat Styrofoam sheet onto tracing paper.

3. Draw your poster on the tracing paper. Doodle large letters to make them easy to read!

4. Flip the tracing paper around so that the words read backward. Lay it flat on top of your Styrofoam sheet. Trace over your letters and drawing. Press your pencil hard to make an impression on the Styrofoam, but not so hard that it pokes a hole through it!

Helpful Tip: Tape your tracing paper to stop it from shifting while you trace.

CONTINUED

5. Pour a thin layer of paint onto a plastic plate or tray. Coat your sponge roller with paint and roll the paint onto your Styrofoam sheet.

6. Lay down a sheet of cardstock. Flip the paint side of the Styrofoam sheet onto the cardstock and rub, rub, rub! Lift the Styrofoam up gently. Set aside to let the paint dry for 30 minutes.

7. Continue to roll more paint onto the Styrofoam sheet and stamp more posters on cardstock. Lay them out and let each one dry for 30 minutes.

8. Tape up your posters to spread your news!

FUN FACT: One of Shepard Fairey's most famous artworks is a poster of President Barack Obama with the word *hope*. It became a symbol of Obama's 2008 presidential campaign. The original poster is at the Smithsonian Institution.

S T E A M CONNECTION: Did you know there's a machine that rolls and stamps just like you did in this project? The invention is called the printing press! The one first designed by Johannes Gutenberg could print 3,600 sheets in a day. How many do you think you could print in a day?

NOW TRY THIS!

➤ Play with negative and positive space by pressing your pencil into the opposite space on your Styrofoam. Instead of tracing on the lines (**positive space**), try rubbing the pencil in the empty (**negative space**) areas.

➤ Try it with craft foam stickers! Instead of drawing, try sticking the foam stickers to a sheet of Styrofoam to create a pattern. Roll on paint and stamp!

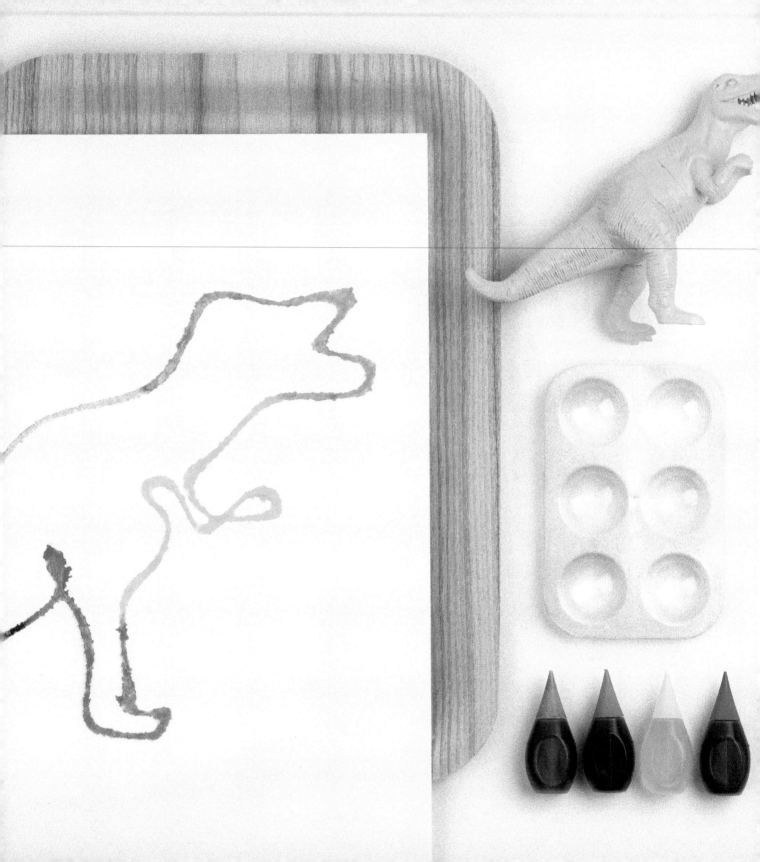

OUTLINE A FORM

TIME: 60 MINUTES

DIFFICULTY LEVEL: MEDIUM

MEDIUM: FOOD COLORING, GLUE, AND SALT ON PAPER

TECHNIQUE: CONTINUOUS CONTOUR LINE, RAISED SALT PAINTING

MATERIALS

- Toy
- Watercolor or cardstock paper
- White school glue
- Table salt
- Serving tray
- Paint palette or an ice cube tray
- Teaspoon
- Cup of water
- Food coloring in red, yellow, blue, and green
- Pipette or eye dropper

Have you heard of a continuous line or a **contour** drawing? It's a technique an artist uses to practice outlining **forms** with a single line. Artists do this to help train their observation skills. Typically, an artist will use a pencil to practice making their line. In this project, we'll add some fun with a squeeze of glue and a sprinkle of salt!

 CAUTION: Food coloring may stain fingers, surfaces, and clothing. Be sure to protect your art space and wear an apron.

THE STEPS

1. Stand or lay the toy next to your sheet of paper. Follow the outline of the toy with your eyes as practice. This is how an artist studies an object they plan to draw.

2. To begin drawing, squeeze the glue onto the paper at the same time as your eyes follow along the outline of your toy.

CONTINUED

Keep your eyes on the toy, and don't look down at your paper. Move the glue bottle at the same speed and direction as you feel your eyes move. Stop when you think you've gone all the way around the toy with your eyes. How does your line look? A little wonky? Perfect! A contour line drawing is for practice anyway, so let's enjoy the rest of the project with salt and paint!

3. Sprinkle salt all over your sheet of paper to make it stick to the glue line.

4. Shake off the leftover salt onto a serving tray for easy cleanup. Leave your art to dry for 30 minutes.

5. Spoon ¼ teaspoon or ½ teaspoon of water into each pod of your palette or ice cube tray. Add one to four drops of food coloring to each pod.

6. Play with mixing colors. Mix red, yellow, green, and blue to make new colors. Fill as many pods as you want!

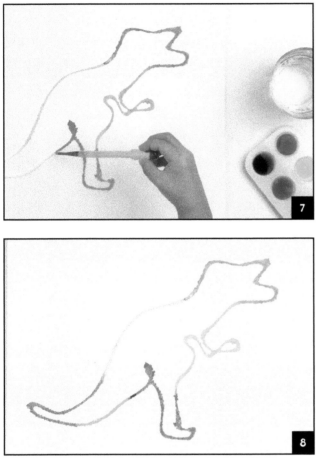

7. Fill a pipette with one color. Drop one tiny dot of color onto the dried salt line. Watch the color move across the line. Empty and rinse out your pipette into a cup of water before switching to the next color. Continue adding drops of color along the salt line.

8. Leave it to dry for 30 minutes and then hang it on your wall to display!

> **FUN FACT:** One artist named Differantly (DFT) became so well recognized for his continuous line art that his designs were printed onto Nike sneakers!

STEAM CONNECTION: Did you know salt is hygroscopic? That means it can attract and absorb water, and it's why the watercolor drops spread along only the salt line in this project.

NOW TRY THIS!

➤ Does the paper matter? Try this project with different kinds of paper and make a note of which papers pucker and which ones create the crispest line.

➤ The next time you study your object, pay attention to the light and shadows. Squeeze the glue harder when you see shadows and squeeze more gently when you see more light on the outline of your toy. What do you notice?

MIX UP COLORS

TIME: 30 MINUTES
DIFFICULTY LEVEL: MEDIUM
MEDIUM: CARDBOARD, MARKER, WOODEN STICK, AND PAPER
TECHNIQUE: SUBTRACTIVE COLOR MIXING

MATERIALS

- White cardstock paper (8 ½ inches × 11 inches)
- Circular object to trace (about 2 inches in diameter)
- Pencil
- Ruler
- Markers in red, yellow, and blue
- Cardboard
- Glue stick
- Toothpick
- Safety scissors

Did you know you can mix an endless number of colors with just red, yellow, and blue (RYB)? This trio is called the **primary colors**. Artists use these colors to mix paint, markers, and inks to make their art. Here, we'll spin to mix primary colors to see what new colors appear!

CAUTION: Toothpicks and other objects used to pierce holes into the cardboard are sharp and can hurt fingers or eyes. Grown-ups are needed to supervise steps 6 and 7.

THE STEPS

1. Trace six circles on the cardstock.

2. Measure the circle's diameter and divide the number in half to find the center point. Mark a dot in the center of the circle. Repeat for all circles.

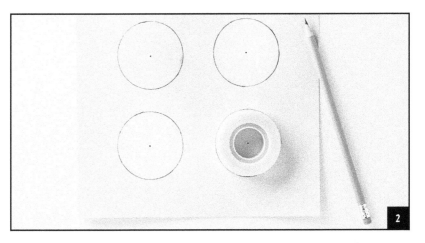

CONTINUED

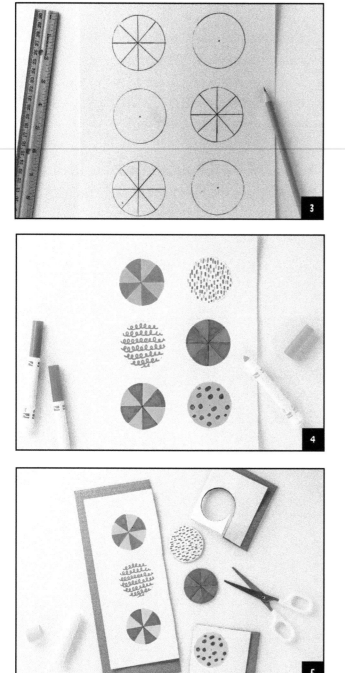

3. Draw an × through one of the circles. Draw a + through the same circle. Repeat this eight-piece pie design for as many circles as you wish.

4. Color in the circles using your primary markers: red, yellow, and blue. Doodling different patterns can work, too.

5. Glue the backside of the paper onto a sheet of cardboard from a used box. Cut out each circle.

6. Pierce the center dot of the circle with a toothpick. To make sure you keep your fingers safe, lay the circle on top of a scrap sheet of cardboard on a table before pushing the toothpick in. If the toothpick breaks, ask an adult to use a sharp pencil or a needle to make a tiny hole.

7. Snip off about ½ inch of the toothpick very carefully. Hold the end being snipped off so that it doesn't fly away. Keep scissors away from your fingertips.

8. Spin the tops using your thumb and index fingers to twirl the toothpick and let it go! What colors appear?

> **FUN FACT:** When you mix two primary colors, you get a **secondary color**, and if you mix a primary with a secondary, you get a **tertiary color**.

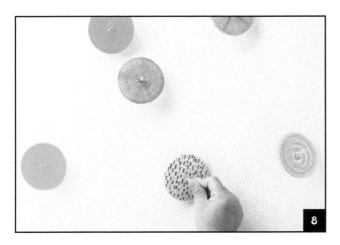

⬤ⓉⒻⒶⓂ **CONNECTION:** Physicist James David Forbes and mathematician James Clerk Maxwell used spinning tops to show the perception of color. Scientists observe color as a light spectrum, where red, green, and blue (RGB) are the primaries for **additive colors** because when mixed they make white. For artists, colors are observed as pigments, and the colors RYB are the primaries for **subtractive colors** because when mixed they make black.

NOW TRY THIS!

➲ Printers use cyan, magenta, and yellow to make an endless range of colors. Try them for your spin tops and see what new colors appear.

➲ Divide colors into 4-piece pies or 12-piece pies. Does the color mix better or worse than the 8-piece-pie design?

SHADE WITH DOTS

TIME: 60 MINUTES
DIFFICULTY LEVEL: MEDIUM
MEDIUM: ACRYLIC ON CANVAS PANEL
TECHNIQUE: STIPPLING, DRAWING 3D FORMS

MATERIALS

- Canvas panel or cardstock paper
- Acrylic paint in light pink, dark pink, and yellow
- Paint palette or ice cube tray
- Cup of water
- Flat paintbrush
- Toy cheese wedge, cake slice, or triangle building block
- Pencil
- Eraser
- Cotton swabs

Let's make 3D-style art with dots! **3D**-style art uses height, width, and depth to trick the eyes into thinking a flat painting is popping out of the canvas. Here, we'll learn a technique called stippling to paint a 3D cheese wedge.

CAUTION: Acrylic paint is not washable. Be sure to protect your art space and wear an apron.

THE STEPS

1. Find a spot near a window to set up your art space. You will be using sunlight to help study light and shadows. In these photos, the window is on the left-hand side.

2. Paint the whole canvas with light pink acrylic paint. Use left and right strokes only. Let it dry for 20 minutes. If you're painting on paper, skip to step 4.

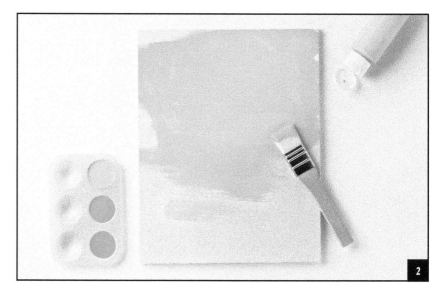

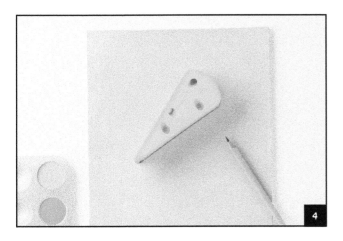

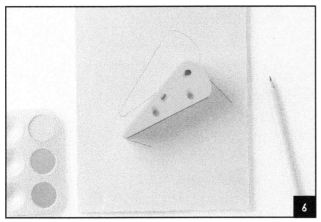

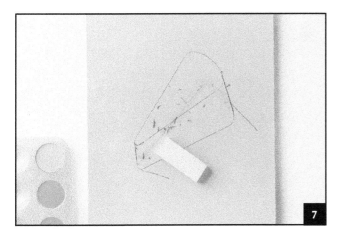

3. Paint a second layer of light pink acrylic, this time using up-and-down strokes. This is how artists prepare their base layer of paint on canvas. The crisscrossed layers mimic the fabric of the canvas. Let it dry for 20 more minutes.

4. Place your triangle block on the canvas and trace around it very lightly with a pencil.

5. Slide the block down three finger spaces (about 1½ inches) and retrace the shape very lightly.

6. Study the color of the block. Which sides of the block are lighter? Which sides are darker? How large is the shadow on the canvas? Trace the shadow line very lightly.

Helpful Tip: Turn off the lights in your space to see a clearer single source of sunlight from the window.

7. Remove the block and draw a line that connects the top triangle to the bottom triangle shape. Erase the inner line as shown in the photo.

CONTINUED

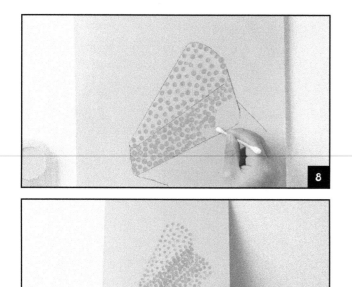

8. Dip a cotton swab in yellow paint and add dots to the top triangle shape. Leave some space between the dots. Continue to paint dots until it is filled in. Earlier, you noticed the darker side of the block. Paint that side with dots closer together, touching, or overlapping slightly.

9. Dip a new cotton swab in dark pink paint and add dots to the shadow of the block. As you paint farther away to the outside edges of the shadow, use fewer dots, and spread them out. Let the paint dry for 30 minutes.

10. Gently erase the pencil lines. Display your artwork and stand back to look. What do you notice? Do you see the 3D effect of stippling?

FUN FACT: Cheese inspires art! Clara Peeters painted **still-life** cheese, Salvador Dalí mimicked melted cheese, and Jim Victor and Sarah Kaufmann sculpt with cheese!

CONNECTION: Impressionist painter Georges Seurat explored optic science, the study of light, to inspire a style he called **pointillism**. Like our cheese painting, the dots in his paintings are used to play with light and shadows.

NOW TRY THIS!
- Test a new shape, maybe one with a curve, like a can of soup.
- Get inspired by pointillism and add more colors!

DESIGN WITH RHYTHM

TIME: 30 MINUTES

DIFFICULTY LEVEL: MEDIUM

MEDIUM: LED LIGHTS, FELT, AND CARDBOARD TUBES

TECHNIQUE: UPCYCLING

MATERIALS

- Cardstock paper (8 ½ inches × 11 inches)
- Pencil
- Ruler
- Safety scissors
- Hole punch
- 5 LED tealights
- 5 cardboard tubes (from paper towel or toilet paper rolls)
- Washi tape or Scotch tape
- 1 round shoelace or parachute cord
- 5 Eco-fi felt sheets or any new or reused felt sheets in any color
- Fabric glue, or hot glue gun with sticks
- Clothespin

One of the principles of art and design is **rhythm**. Rhythm can be heard in music, or it can be seen in art. Rhythm can be seen through patterns using shapes, colors, lines, or forms. Let's learn to design with rhythm by making your own luminary!

CAUTION: Button batteries inside LED tealights are a choking hazard and toxic when swallowed. Grown-ups must ensure the batteries are secured inside the candle and not easily accessible to children.

THE STEPS

1. Lay the sheet of cardstock with the longer side running horizontally. Draw three vertical lines on the cardstock, 1 inch apart. Draw one horizontal line across the center of the page. Cut along the lines to make four (4¼ inch × 1 inch) strips. You will end up with six strips, but you'll only need to use five.

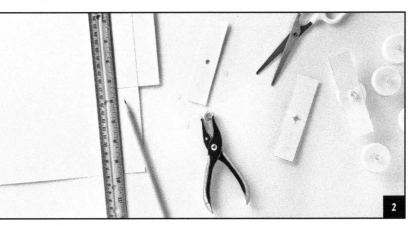

CONTINUED

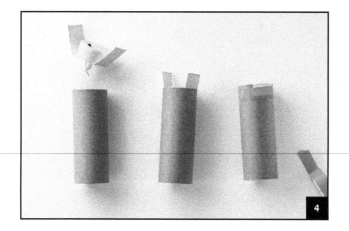

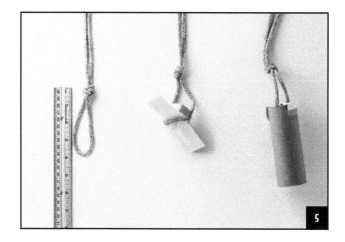

2. Using the hole punch, punch a hole at the center of each strip. Using scissors, notch a crosshair (+) through the punched hole as shown. Repeat for each strip.

3. Pierce the "flame" of one tealight through the hole. Repeat for all the tealights.

4. Fold the strip around the tealight and place it into one cardboard tube, "flame"-side down. Fold over the strip and tape both sides of the strip to the outside of the tube. Repeat for the next three tealights.

5. Fold a shoelace in half and tie a knot to make a 3- to 4-inch-diameter loop. Tape the bottom of the loop to the paper of the last tealight. Fold the paper around the tealight and insert into the tube. Fold over the strip and tape it to the tube as shown in the photo.

6. Lay a cardboard tube onto a sheet of felt, making sure to line it up to the edge. With a ruler against the other edge of the tube, draw a line down the sheet. Cut along the line.

7. Glue the felt onto the tube using fabric glue or a hot glue gun. Cut off any remaining felt. Repeat steps 6 and 7 for all remaining tubes.

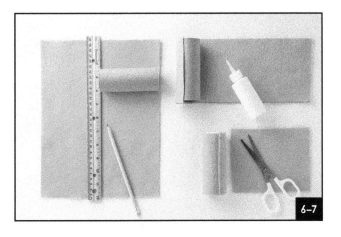

8. Play with the arrangement of the finished tubes. There are different types of rhythms you can create: You can design a regular rhythm by lining up the tubes together in a neat row; an alternating rhythm by creating an up-and-down pattern; a progressive rhythm by arranging the tubes as steps; or a random rhythm by placing them any way you'd like. Keep balance in mind. Make sure you plan the center tube to be the one with the shoelace to keep your luminary balanced.

9. Once you've planned your design, glue together the finished tubes. Use clothespins and/or tape to keep them in place until the glue dries for about an hour. Remove the clothespins and tape when dried.

10. Flip on the switch for each tealight and hang your design! You can hang your luminary on your doorknob and use it as a night light.

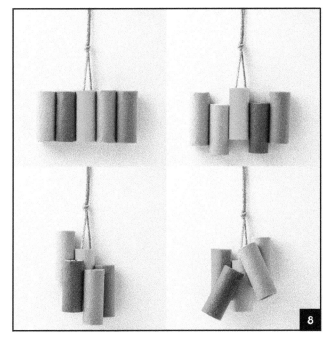

CONTINUED

FUN FACT: Did you know there are architects famous for the luminaries they've designed? The PH Artichoke by Poul Henningsen is a famous light fixture with leaves that layer downward in a progressive rhythm.

STEAM CONNECTION: Can we hear rhythm through our eyes? Neuroscientists are exploring abstract painter Wassily Kandinsky's experience seeing sound in different colors. What do you think? What color would a trumpet make?

NOW TRY THIS!

- Add more tubes! Make it bigger!
- Add pom-poms to each tube. What kind of rhythm do they add?

MELT WAX AND MAKE ART

TIME: 45 MINUTES

DIFFICULTY LEVEL: MEDIUM

MEDIUM: WAX, CUT-AND-PASTED PAPER ON WOOD PANEL

TECHNIQUE: WAX PAINTING

MATERIALS

- Colored cardstock or construction paper
- Pencil
- Paper bowl
- Ruler
- Safety scissors
- 12 wax crayons in shades of blue or in rainbow colors
- Recycled cardboard
- Wood panel (12 inches × 12 inches or larger)
- Washi tape or masking tape
- Newspaper
- Blow-dryer
- White school glue

What's a new way to use crayons in your artwork? By melting them, of course! Here, we'll have some fun making it rain and expressing how a rainy day feels to you with an umbrella caricature.

CAUTION: Hot wax will splatter, stain, and burn. Be sure to protect your art space and wear an apron. Wear long sleeves and gloves for added protection.

Helpful Tip: Leftover broken crayons are perfect for this activity!

THE STEPS

1. Draw an umbrella shape on the colored cardstock. Follow the example and trace the paper bowl and use a ruler to make the umbrella shape and handle. Cut out both pieces and set them aside.

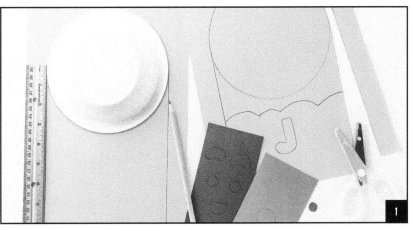

CONTINUED

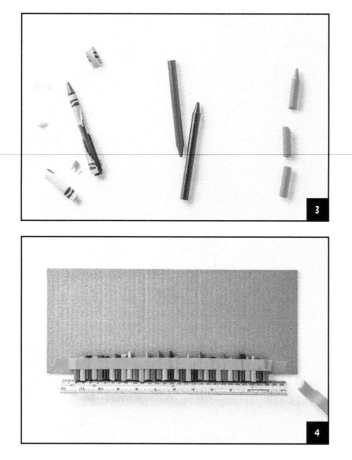

2. Reflect on how the rain makes you feel. Do you feel joy? Sadness? Love? Boredom? Think of the facial expression the feeling would show. Draw eyes, eyebrows, a nose, and a mouth to match that expression on a different sheet of colored cardstock. Cut out all the shapes and set them aside.

3. Peel off the paper from each of the crayons. Break each crayon into three pieces.

4. Line up the crayons on a piece of cardboard as wide as your wooden panel. The cardboard can be slightly wider than your wooden panel. Be sure to overhang the crayons about ½ inch from the bottom of the cardboard. Use a ruler to help straighten the bottom of the crayons. Tape the crayons securely into place.

5. Tape the paper bowl to the middle of the wooden panel. Secure the tape over the center of the bowl and around the back of the wood panel—make sure the tape isn't touching the front of the panel.

6. Lean the wooden panel against a wall. Be sure to protect the wall with a large sheet of newspaper. Place your crayons on top of the wooden panel. You may need to tape the cardboard to the wall to stop it from falling.

7. Melt the crayons with a blow-dryer using high heat. Wait 15 minutes for the wax to cool.

8. Remove the paper bowl and the crayons attached to the cardboard.

9. Glue your cut umbrella shape in the space made by the bowl. Glue the eyes, nose, mouth, and eyebrows to make the expression you drew earlier.

10. Hang on your wall and enjoy!

FUN FACT: Encaustic paintings are melted wax paintings just like yours! Many can be found in history; the oldest is from Egypt, dating back to 100 to 300 CE.

STEAM CONNECTION: The earliest wax art was made with beeswax. Young honeybees "sweat" out liquid beeswax from their bellies. Once it comes out, it hardens, and bees mold the wax with their jaws to create honeycombs to store their honey. Without bees, we might have never had crayons! The next time you see one, thank the little insect!

NOW TRY THIS!
- Take your art outside! Melt the crayons on a hot summer's day. Use sticks to smear the wax.
- Cover a wooden panel with melted wax. After the wax has cooled, carve a picture with a plastic knife or ice pop stick!

EXPRESS IT WITH PIXELS

TIME: 60 MINUTES
DIFFICULTY LEVEL: MEDIUM
MEDIUM: STICKY NOTES ON A WALL
TECHNIQUE: PIXEL ART, MURAL GRID METHOD

MATERIALS

- Grid paper (page 108)
- Colored pencils in yellow, blue, and red (erasable preferred)
- Measuring tape
- Safety scissors
- String in green and blue
- Sticky note pads, 144 sheets (about 124 yellow, 8 blue, 12 red)
- Washi tape or painter's tape

What do our faces show when we're feeling mad, happy, or silly? Can you say what you're feeling with an emoji (絵文字)? An emoji is a tiny cartoon made of **pixels** used with text to express an emotion, like this: 😄. Did you know the first emoji designs were made up of 144 pixels? Here, we'll design our own with sticky notes as our pixels to express feelings.

Helpful Tip: Sticky notes may fall off easily if the walls are not smooth. If this happens, try this project on a large window, mirror, or white board. Another option is to use a sticky notepad that is labeled "super-sticky."

THE STEPS

1. Plan your emoji using grid paper. Color in a few squares with a yellow pencil to create an outline of a circle for your emoji face. Begin in one quarter of the grid and continue around the sheet.

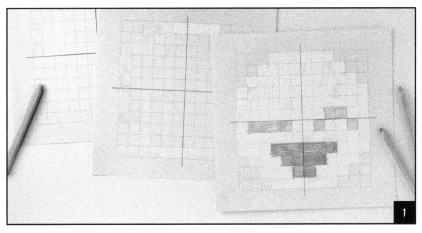

CONTINUED

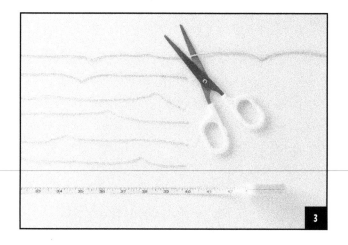

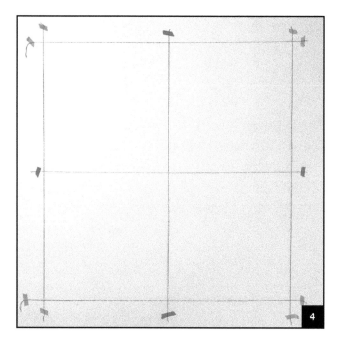

2. Think about how you're feeling. How do you express it with your face? Color in eyes with a blue pencil and red for the mouth. Choose any facial expression you're feeling or want to make. Fill in the leftover squares of the face with yellow.

3. Measure and cut 40 inches of blue string four times and 40 inches of green string two times.

4. Find a blank wall (36 inches × 36 inches) for you to install your art. The smoother the wall, the better! Stick three notes on your wall to test if they stay up. Be sure to rub the top of the note down well. Take down the notes after testing. Tape up the two green strings like a plus sign (+) in the middle of the wall. Tape up the four blue strings around the plus sign, 18 inches away from the green lines. These four quadrants or squares will be your guide for putting up the sticky notes.

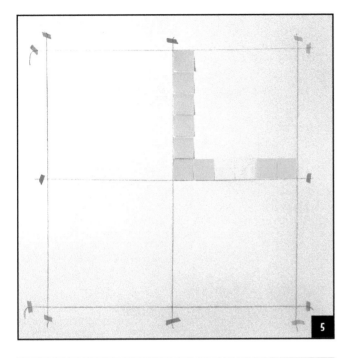

5. Starting from the middle, place the sticky notes on the wall. Follow the green line and use your grid paper drawing to guide you on which colors to use. Don't worry about matching up the sticky notes perfectly. Move the notes around if you run out of space. Remember, your artwork isn't permanent; it's okay to redo parts here and there.

6. Fill the rest of the quadrant and then move to the next, starting again from the green line in the center. Keep checking your grid paper to guide you.

7. Step back to enjoy your creation!

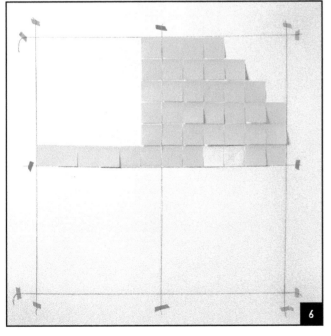

CONTINUED

FUN FACT: The first emojis were designed by Shigetaka Kurita. Today, they can be found at the Museum of Modern Art (MoMA) in New York.

STEAM CONNECTION: Pixels, or tiny squares, are what computers use to display images. Every image we see on a screen is made up of thousands of pixels. The first pixel image was a scanned photo in 1957 by computer scientist Russell Kirsch. That image was a baby photo of his child. How cute is that?

NOW TRY THIS!

- Ask a grown-up if you can cover an entire wall to create a mural.
- Choose new colors or make a unicorn or hand emoji! Let your creativity loose!
- Stick it on your window! Send a message to your neighbors with a pixel design. Who will respond?

ANIMATE A DOODLE

TIME: 30 MINUTES

DIFFICULTY LEVEL: MEDIUM

MEDIUM: MARKER ON PAPER

TECHNIQUE: FLIPBOOK ANIMATION

MATERIALS

- At least 20 index cards or cardstock cut to size (3 inches × 5 inches)
- Pencil
- Markers in two shades of brown
- Smartphone or tablet
- Large binder clip

If a cookie could feel itself being eaten, what would it do? Maybe it starts off as feeling happy and then . . . *CHOMP!* The cookie is shocked and then . . . *CHOMP!* Would the cookie feel worried next? Let's doodle your ideas and see what happens when we bring your ideas to life with a flipbook!

Helpful Tip: It's easier to trace an image when you have light behind your paper. You can try holding your paper against a sunlit window or on top of a smartphone or tablet. If you're using an electronic device, ask a grown-up to save a photo of a white background and display it with maximum brightness on the screen. You can also create your own lightbox by drawing on top of a closed, clear storage box with a lit flashlight inside.

THE STEPS

1. Number the back corner of each index card (1, 2, 3, 4, and so forth) with a pencil to keep track of the order of the cards.

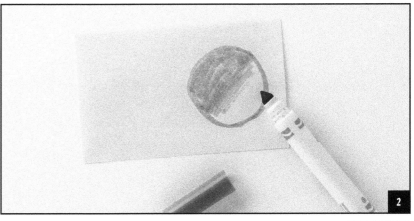

CONTINUED

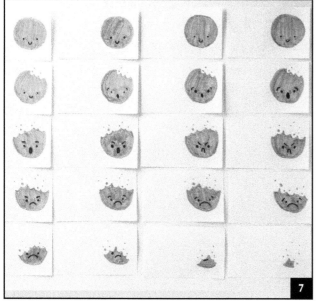

2. On card 1, using the light brown marker, draw a circle on one index card near the right side of the sheet. This is your cookie. Using the dark brown marker, doodle a smiley face near the bottom of the circle.

3. Place card 1 on your smartphone, tablet, or homemade lightbox and lay card 2 on top. Be sure to line up the edges of the paper to match.

4. Trace the cookie you see through the card. Begin with the smiley face this time, then the circle, and color it in. Set card 1 aside.

5. Place card 3 on top of card 2 and repeat step 4. Set aside card 2. Place card 4 on top of card 3 and repeat step 4. Set aside card 3.

6. On card 5, trace the smiley face from card 4; then trace **most** of the circle, and draw a bite mark into the top right of the cookie. Add dots as crumbs. Set aside card 4.

7. Continue to trace and doodle on cards 6 to 20 using the photo here to guide you on the sequence. The cards are laid out here in order of left to right, top to bottom.

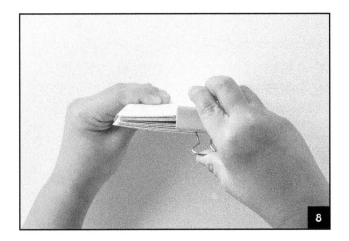

8. Order your cards from 1 to 20, stacking them from front to back. Tap your cards on their sides to align them neatly. Be sure to tap on the right side of the paper last and hold it together with a binder clip on the left side of the stack.

9. Flip through the pages using your thumb and see your image move!

FUN FACT: Ruth Wakefield invented the first chocolate chip cookie around 1938, and her recipe can still be found on the back of a Nestlé Toll House chocolate chip bag.

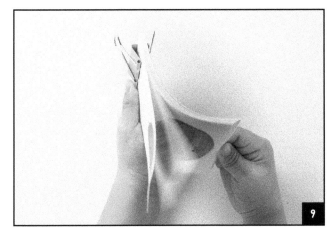

STEAM CONNECTION: Digital animations like a GIF (graphics interchange format) work the same way as flipbooks do. In a GIF, each "page" is called a frame. GIFs can have a framerate of 15 to 30 fps (frames per second). When you play each frame really quickly, you get an animation, just like a flipbook!

NOW TRY THIS!

→ How would a glass of milk react if someone drank it all up? Animate your idea!

→ Doodle more pages! How many pages can you add to a flipbook?

SCRIBBLE WITH A BOT

TIME: 60 MINUTES
DIFFICULTY LEVEL: MEDIUM
MEDIUM: MARKER
ON PAPER
TECHNIQUE: PROCESS ART

MATERIALS

- Empty tissue box
- 3 sheets of colored cardstock or construction paper
- Pencil
- Ruler
- Safety scissors
- Glue stick
- Loose parts (bottle caps, straws, pom-poms, etc.)
- Hot glue gun and glue sticks
- Easel paper roll
- Toy remote-control car
- Washable markers
- Washi tape or masking tape

Can you make a mega loop, zigzag, or wavy line? How about a super line longer than your body! How would you do it? What if you had a robot to help you? Artists sometimes use machines to help create their art. Would you like to try it?

CAUTION: Hot glue will burn. Do not touch the nozzle of the glue gun or the hot glue until cooled. Younger kids must ask grown-ups to use the hot glue gun. Low-temperature hot glue guns are available at craft stores for older kids.

THE STEPS

1. Place the empty tissue box on a sheet of cardstock, leaving a ½-inch border around the box. If the sheet needs to be smaller, draw a line and cut along it.

2. Trace around the bottom of the box on the same sheet. Add diagonal lines to the corners and snip off the corners.

3. Trace along the smallest side of the box on a new sheet. Draw a parallel line next to the shortest sides (outside of the box), about ½ inch away. Cut along the outside lines only. Repeat to make a second sheet.

4. Trace the longest sides of the box on a new sheet two times, and cut along the lines.

5. Fold along all pencil lines remaining on each sheet for all of the cut pieces.

6. Cut out the top of the tissue box.

7. Glue the largest piece to the bottom of the tissue box. Glue on the smallest sides. Glue on the longest sides.

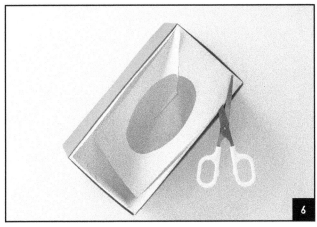

CONTINUED

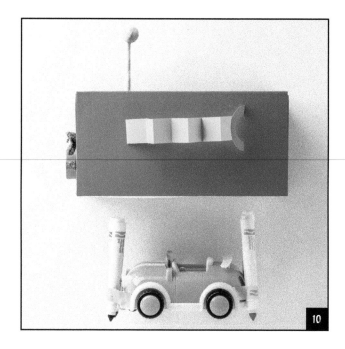

8. The paper-covered box is the body of your robot! Hot glue loose parts to it to decorate it. You can also add arms with folded paper. Use your imagination!

9. Lay down a roll of easel paper on the floor to create a robot doodle zone.

Helpful Tip: Lay down many strips of paper along a hallway. Be sure to block off the edges of the paper with boxes to stop the robot from getting out.

10. Tape markers to the front and back of your remote-control car, as shown in the photo. Be sure to take the caps off and have the marker tips point down to touch the paper on the floor. Turn on your car if there's a switch.

11. Cover your remote-control car with your robot.

12. Use your remote to create different types of lines!

FUN FACT: Have you heard of Ai-Da? She's the first robot artist! She was named after Ada Lovelace, the first computer programmer!

⬤**T**⬤**A**⬤ **CONNECTION:** **A new movement in art is rising. A wave of artists is creating with artificial intelligence (AI). This blend of art and technology is called neural network art!**

NOW TRY THIS!
➔ Try writing your name across the easel paper to create a banner.
➔ Make another scribble bot by taping markers to an electric toothbrush!

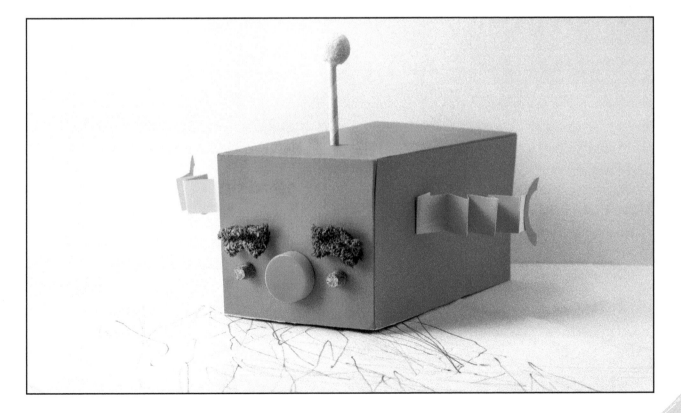

REIMAGINE CRUMPLED PAPER

TIME: 60 MINUTES +

DIFFICULTY LEVEL: CHALLENGING

MEDIUM: PAPIER-MÂCHÉ, ACRYLIC, AND LOOSE PARTS

TECHNIQUE: SCULPTING, PAPIER-MÂCHÉ

MATERIALS

- Large plastic grocery bag
- Masking tape (¾ inch thick)
- Recycled sheet of paper
- Newspaper or newsprint
- ¼ cup warm water
- ¼ cup white glue (or 1 tablespoon salt and 2 tablespoons flour)
- Small mixing bowl
- Small whisk or fork
- Art drying rack, parchment paper, or a cooling rack
- Paper straws

CONTINUED

Have you ever crumpled up and tossed out a drawing that didn't come out perfect? What if I told you that we could turn that paper into art? In this project, we'll reimagine crumpled paper with a sculpting technique called **papier-mâché** (chewed paper), and we'll turn it into a fun character with a bit of imagination!

 CAUTION: Hot glue will burn. Do not touch the nozzle of the glue gun or the hot glue until cooled. Younger kids must ask grown-ups to use the hot glue gun. Low-temperature hot glue guns are available for older kids.

THE STEPS

1. Cover your table with a large plastic grocery bag to protect it from spills and drips. Cut the bag open to unfold it. Tape it down to your work surface with masking tape.

2. Crumple up a recycled sheet of paper to form a blob-like shape. Wrap the entire blob with masking tape. Set aside.

MATERIALS (CONT.)

- ➔ Scrap cardstock paper
- ➔ Safety scissors
- ➔ Hot glue gun and glue sticks
- ➔ Acrylic paint
- ➔ Paintbrushes
- ➔ Cup of water
- ➔ Paint rag or wipes
- ➔ Loose parts (pom-poms, string, googly eyes, etc.)

3. Tear about half the newspaper into long 1-inch-wide strips. Then tear the strips into smaller rectangular pieces, some about 2 inches × 1 inch and others about 1 inch × ½ inch. Set aside your two piles.

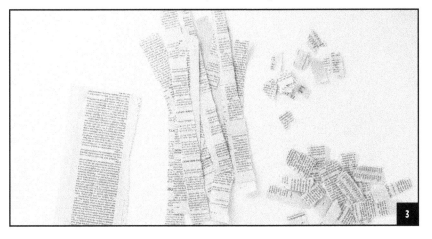

Helpful Tip: Newsprint will tear into long strips easily. If you're having trouble, try tearing in a different direction.

4. Mix the warm water and white glue together in a bowl to make the papier-mâché paste.

Helpful Tip: If you don't have white glue, mix 1 tablespoon of salt with ¼ cup of warm water until the granules are dissolved. Then mix in 2 tablespoons of flour until smooth.

5. Dip one torn piece of newsprint into the paste. Lift out the piece while touching the side of the bowl to remove any excess paste.

CONTINUED

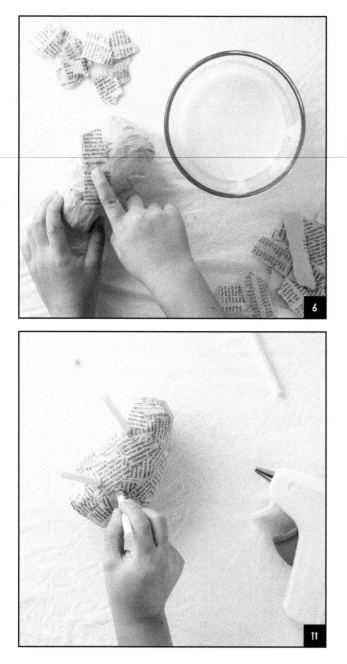

6. Lay the paper flat onto your blob and smooth out the paper by rubbing with your fingers gently in a circular motion.

7. Repeat steps 5 and 6 while overlapping each piece of torn newsprint by about half. Use the larger pile of torn newsprint for flatter surfaces and use the smaller pieces for more curved surfaces on the blob. Continue until the whole blob is covered.

8. Rub down any crinkles or lifted edges as much as possible. If some crinkles don't stay flat after rubbing, add one small piece of torn newsprint to help keep them down.

9. Dry the blob on a rack or on parchment paper and turn it over each day. Drying may take 2 to 3 days. Touch the blob each day. If it feels wet, cold, or soft, it will need another day to dry.

10. Play with your blob. What do you see? Turn it around, stand it upside down, toss it in the air, and see where it lands. Does it inspire you to create something? You can hot glue on paper straws and cut paper to add details to bring your imagination to life! Add legs, arms, horns, ears, or a tail.

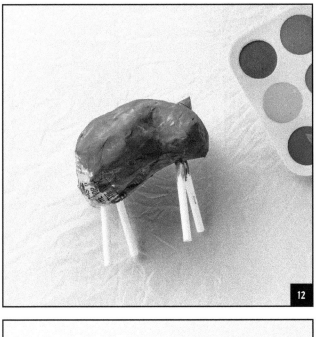

11. Balance may be tricky to create with this blob because of its irregular shape. To add legs with paper straws, be sure to add one leg at a time with a pea-size dot of hot glue. Hold one straw leg in place until the hot glue is cooled down. When the hot glue turns foggy or milky, it's cooled down. Move on to adding the next leg in the same way. After adding all the legs, trim them with scissors a little at a time, checking for balance after each snip.

Helpful Tip: Hot glue can make a stringy mess if you don't use it properly. To stop the strings, make small circular motions with the hot glue gun while pulling away ½ inch from the glue dot. Once you see the string break, you can set your hot glue gun down.

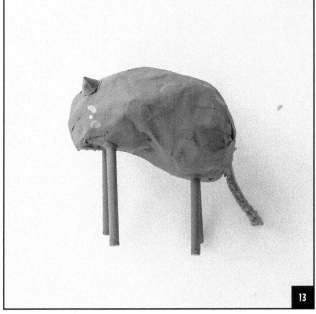

12. Brush on one coat (layer) of paint. Leave it to dry for 20 minutes. Repeat with another coat of paint until the letters from the newsprint don't show through. Lighter colors might need up to three coats of paint.

13. Glue on pom-poms, string, or googly eyes for extra fun!

CONTINUED

FUN FACT: Artist duo Adam Frezza & Terri Chiao (a.k.a. Chiaozza) create papier-mâché artworks, like their *Lump Nubbins* series, from their studio paper scraps!

● ❶ ❶ ❶ ● CONNECTION: In algebra, balance is when two sides of an equation equal the other. For example, 1 + 1 = 2. The value on the left of the equal sign is the same as the value on the right. In art, sculptors and architects play with balance in the same way to create their designs, just like you did here!

NOW TRY THIS!

❯ Stack several painted blobs together as tall as you can! What creation do you see? Hot glue them together and let your imagination inspire what loose parts you might add!

❯ Write an inspirational word or quote on your blob characters and hide them around your home or school to remind you or someone new that inspiration can come from anywhere.

PAINT DEPTH WITH COLOR

TIME: 60 MINUTES +

DIFFICULTY LEVEL: CHALLENGING

MEDIUM: TEMPERA PAINT, CORRECTION FLUID, AND CHALK ON CUT-AND-PASTED PAPER

TECHNIQUE: FLAT WASH, AERIAL PERSPECTIVE, MIXING TINTS AND SHADES

MATERIALS

- 2 sheets watercolor paper (300 gsm [140 lb.], 9 inches × 12 inches)
- Pencil
- Ruler
- Drawing board or easel, on a 30-degree angle
- Washi tape or ½-inch masking tape
- Paint rag or paper towel
- Cup of water
- Small bowl of water or a second cup

Let's learn how to tint and shade colors to paint rolling hills that drift off into the distance! In this project, we'll play with a technique called **aerial perspective (or atmospheric perspective)**. This technique is what artists use to paint the effect of **depth**, or the feeling of distance. Ready to mix some paint and give this effect a try?

Helpful Tip: Place two soda cans under a wood painting panel to create an angled drawing board.

THE STEPS

1. Lay your watercolor paper with the longest side of the sheet running horizontally.

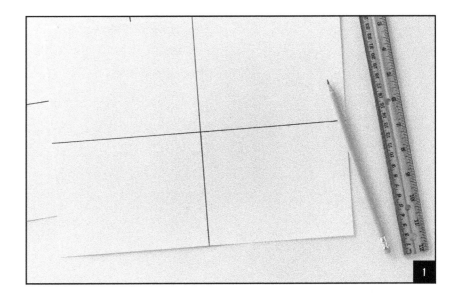

CONTINUED

CONTINUED

MATERIALS (CONT.)

- Round paintbrush, size 14 or larger, about as thick as your pinky finger
- Tempera cakes or water-color pan in blue and orange
- Mixing palette or ice cube tray
- Scrap white paper
- Safety scissors
- Glue stick
- Correction fluid pen or white acrylic paint with a thin, rounded brush
- White chalk

2. Draw a vertical line across the middle of your sheet. To do this, use a ruler and draw a dot at the top of the paper, 6 inches away from the left edge. Then repeat at the bottom of the paper. Connect the dots with a vertical line.

3. Draw a horizontal line across the middle of your sheet. To do this, use a ruler and draw a dot on the left side of the paper, measuring down 4½ inches from the top. Then repeat at the right side of the paper. Connect the dots with a horizontal line.

4. Repeat steps 1 to 3 with your second sheet of watercolor paper.

5. Tape the four edges of one sheet of paper to a drawing board with washi tape. Tape over the pencil lines with washi tape to create four rectangles to paint on.

6. Set up your art space by laying down a paint rag first. Then place a cup of water for rinsing, a small bowl of water for mixing with paint, one blue and one orange tempera cake, and a mixing palette.

7. Dip your brush into the bowl and drop 4 drops of water into a pod on the mixing palette. Repeat with three more pods.

8. Mix the tints. To do this, dip your brush into the bowl and drip 10 waterdrops onto the blue tempera cake. Swirl the brush on the cake to activate the paint. With the paint on the brush:

   a. In pod 1, drip 1 drop of blue paint.
   b. In pod 2, drip 3 drops of blue paint.
   c. In pod 3, drip 6 drops of blue paint.
   d. In pod 4, drip 10 drops of blue paint. Wipe the brush on the towel to dry it off and mix each pod with the brush.

9. Test each tint on a sheet of scrap paper. Each tint should be darker and darker. If not, add more drops of water to lighten the color or drops of blue paint to make it more intense.

10. Flat-wash one of the rectangles with pod 1, the lightest tint. Flat-washing is a technique to cover a large area with paint. Brush the paint across the top of one rectangle. A bead, or a pool of paint, will appear at the bottom of the brush stroke. Make sure this bead runs all the way across the brush stroke. If the bead does not appear or only runs halfway, you can add more paint to your brush and gently tap above where the bead needs to appear to allow some paint to fall.

CONTINUED

11. Brush along the bead line, with each brushstroke moving lower and lower to cover the area with paint. There should always be a bead line at the bottom of your last brushstroke. This will take some practice. Keep going even if it gets a bit messy.

12. Repeat steps 10 and 11 with pods 2, 3, and 4, one rectangle for each pod. Let the paper dry for 20 minutes.

13. Remove the tape and cut each painted rectangle. Trim off any white edges and set aside.

14. Mix the shades. To do this, dip your brush into the bowl and drip 10 waterdrops onto the orange tempera cake. Swirl the brush on the cake to activate the paint. With the paint on the brush, drip 1 drop of orange into each pod of blue tint in the palette. Test your colors on a scrap sheet of paper. Do you notice they turn a little gray and a little darker? This happens when you mix a **complementary color** with a primary color. Orange is the complementary color to blue. Continue to experiment and test your colors to create four different shades of blue.

15. Tape the second sheet of paper and flat-wash the four shades onto the rectangles. Let it dry for 20 minutes.

16. Remove the tape and cut each painted rectangle. Trim off any white edges.

17. Put all eight sheets in order from lightest at the top to darkest at the bottom. The lightest sheets will be used for the **background** (the farthest distance away), and the darkest sheets will be used for the **foreground** (the area closest to you). This is how the effect of depth, or aerial perspective, is done.

18. Doodle some wavy lines to create your rolling hills. Try making a pattern by alternating two hills on one sheet and a single hill on the next sheet. Cut along the wavy lines.

19. Glue the backs of the hills together, overlapping and layering each one as you'd like.

20. Trim the outside edges of your artwork with scissors to make any jagged overlaps neater.

21. Lightly doodle faces and snowcap lines on the hills. Draw over the pencil with a correction fluid pen and chalk.

CONTINUED

22. Stand back and enjoy your artwork. Do you get a sense of depth with your artwork? Do the hills in the background feel farther away?

FUN FACT: One of the world's most famous works of art, the *Mona Lisa*, was painted using this same aerial perspective technique!

🅢🅣🅔🅐🅜 **CONNECTION:** **Why do the hills appear to fade off into the distance? Scientists call it sky radiation. Small air molecules in fog, smoke, or pollution break up and scatter the light, making the hills appear tinted and shaded. In reality, the hills are mostly the same color.**

NOW TRY THIS!

➔ Experiment mixing shades using another primary color and its complementary color from the **color wheel**: red with green and yellow with purple.

➔ Have fun creating new **landscapes**. Make small waves for water, big zigzags for mountain peaks, or small zigzags for trees.

SKETCH A FASHION DESIGN

TIME: 30 MINUTES

DIFFICULTY LEVEL: CHALLENGING

MEDIUM: MARKER ON PAPER

TECHNIQUE: FIGURE DRAWING, FASHION DESIGN

MATERIALS

- Drawing mannequin, doll, or action figure with movable limbs
- Drawing paper
- Pencil
- Tracing paper or parchment paper
- Eraser
- Marker or colored pencils

What color are you wearing today? Does your outfit have patterns, a pocket, or zippers? You may not know that an artist designed the outfit you're wearing. What if you could design your own? Would you add giant buttons, some glitter, or perhaps some rainbow stripes? Let's sketch out some of your fashion ideas!

Helpful Tip: If using parchment paper, use colored pencils instead of markers

THE STEPS

1. Pose your mannequin and lay it next to your drawing paper.

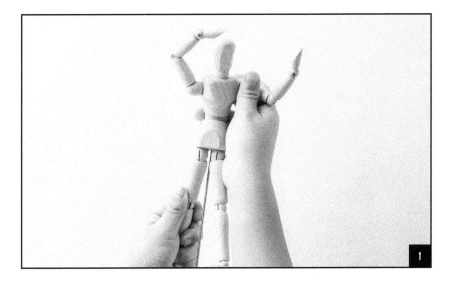

CONTINUED

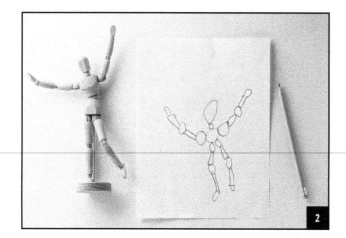

2. Sketch the mannequin. Artists sketch by simplifying forms to basic shapes. Think of this drawing as a template or a skeleton to your final artwork. Be patient and make several sketches.

3. Choose the sketch you're happiest with. Place tracing paper on top and sketch your hair, face, body, and outfit. An eraser is your friend!

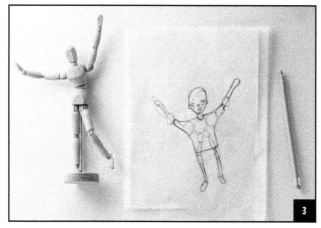

4. Remove the first drawing underneath. Lay another blank sheet of tracing paper on top. Color in your drawing using markers or colored pencils.

5. Design as many outfits as you'd like! Think about different patterns, types of clothing, and textures. Add accessories like a hat, glasses, or a cape! Have fun with your look!

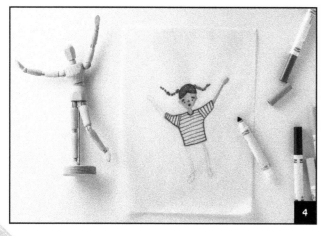

STEAM CONNECTION: Leonardo da Vinci was an artist, engineer, and scientist. His sketch of *The Vitruvian Man* (c. 1490) is a famous example of his knowledge of anatomy, math, and art. The sketch showed how the **proportions** of a man's body can fit into the shape of a circle and a square. Today, we still find the same body proportions on mannequins to help young artists learn to draw.

NOW TRY THIS!

➔ Measure the height of your head with a ruler and cut out an oval matching that size. Can you count how many ovals, or heads, make up your height? Is it five? Six? Or seven? Some artists use the Eight Head Theory to draw the proportions of an adult. How many heads does it take to draw you?

➔ Use dot stickers, glitter pens, and stamps to design your outfit!

SEW WEARABLE ART

TIME: 60 MINUTES +

DIFFICULTY LEVEL: CHALLENGING

MEDIUM: FELT, THREAD, LEDS, AND FOUND OBJECTS

TECHNIQUE: ART-TO-WEAR, E-TEXTILE

MATERIALS

- Measuring tape or string
- Scissors
- Ruler
- Eco-fi felt or any new or reused felt (8 inches long × 20 to 24 inches wide or multiple sheets to make up the length)
- Pencil
- Washi tape or masking tape
- Embroidery thread
- Plastic embroidery needle
- LED string fairy lights (battery-operated)
- Clear tape
- Batteries
- Found objects, such as drinking straws or pony beads
- Hot glue (optional)

Imagine ruling a kingdom. What rules would you create to help make the world a better place? Maybe plant more trees, save on energy, or stop water pollution. Now imagine your crown. Is it green like the trees, yellow like the sun, or blue like the water? Would it be decorated with seeds, light-emitting diodes (LEDs), or plastic straws? Let your mission spark ideas for your **art-to-wear (or wearable art)** crown.

 CAUTION: Needles are sharp! Wear goggles or glasses to prevent poking your eyes, even with a plastic needle.

 CAUTION: Treat the final artwork like any other battery-operated toy. Store at room temperature and keep away from moisture.

THE STEPS

1. Measure the circumference of your head (the length all around your head) using a measuring tape. If using string, ask a grown-up to wrap it around the top of your head and cut. Measure the cut length of your string along a ruler. Write down the number.

2. Skip to step 5 if your single sheet of felt is as long as the circumference of your head. Connect sheets of felt, overlapping by ½ inch. Draw a line using a ruler to help keep overlaps even across several sheets. Tape the

sheets together. Make the tape overlap the seam by ¼ inch. Along the tape, mark little dashes ½ inch apart. The tape and dashes will help you sew neat and even stitches.

3. Cut the width of the connected sheets to match the number you wrote down in step 1, plus 1 inch to make it slightly longer. For example, if you measured 20 inches for your head, then your fabric needs to be 21 inches wide.

4. Backstitch along the taped line(s) to connect the sheets together. To do this, see "How to Sew a Backstitch" on page 88 for step-by-step instructions.

Helpful Tip: Some felts may be too thick for a plastic needle to work. Ask a grown-up to pre-poke holes with a thick metal needle.

5. Fold the felt in half along the short side to make a long strip. Draw a zigzag line across the top, making about seven points. Make sure the peak of one point is at the top of the stitch line. Cut along the zigzag line.

CONTINUED

6. Open up the folded felt. Across the top half of the strip, tape the LED lights on the inside of the felt with clear tape. Look carefully at your stitch line to know which side is the outside (the good side) vs. the inside (bad side). Don't forget to add batteries!

7. Sew or hot glue on decorations, such as cut-up straws. They are sewn on with a single stitch and tied.

8. Fold the felt again as it was in step 5. Backstitch across the top, following the zigzag.

9. Backstitch the ends of the crown together.

10. Wear your art! Let everyone know how you imagine ruling your kingdom to make it a better place!

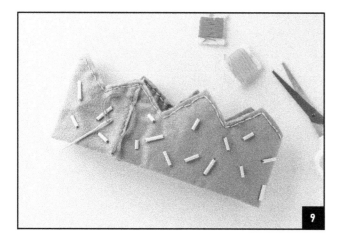

S T E A M CONNECTION: In biology, the top part of the head is called a crown. Humans have three layers in the crown: the skin, skull, and meninges. The job of these layers is to protect our brains! Did royals wear crowns to protect the smartest and the brightest? Hmm . . .

NOW TRY THIS!

➔ Let how you imagine making the world a better place inspire you to use different materials. A crown can be made from cardboard, pipe cleaners, or dandelion flowers.

➔ What if you were a superhero instead? Try making a mask or a cape!

HOW TO SEW A BACKSTITCH

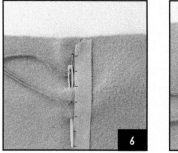

1. Start by threading 40 inches of string through the eye of a needle. Fold the string in half for the ends to meet and make a knot.
2. From the back to the front, poke a hole in the felt next to the first dash at the top. Pull the needle and thread all the way through.
3. From the front to the back, poke the second hole below it. Pull the needle and thread through. This is your first single stitch!
4. Poke a hole next to the third dash. Pull the needle and thread through.
5. Poke back to the second dash and pull the needle and thread through. This is your first backstitch!
6. Poke next to the fourth dash. Pull the needle and thread through. Poke the third dash and pull the needle and thread through. This is your second backstitch!
7. Continue the backstitch all the way down to the bottom of the tape. Remember, you repeat the pattern of poking the next dash forward and then one dash backward. In the end, tie a knot and cut off the leftover string.

COIL A CLAY CUP

TIME: 60 MINUTES +

DIFFICULTY LEVEL: CHALLENGING

MEDIUM: CLAY AND ACRYLIC PAINT

TECHNIQUE: COIL POTTERY, SCORE AND SLIP

MATERIALS

- Easel paper roll or Bristol board paper
- Washi or masking tape
- Air-dry clay, in white
- 2 tablespoons warm water
- Resealable sandwich bag
- Small bowl
- Rolling pin or soda can
- Circular cookie cutter (2 ½ inch diameter) or a cup and butter knife
- Paper bowl (bottom of the bowl must be larger than the cookie cutter)
- Toothpick
- Ice pop stick or wooden stirrer
- Butter knife
- Paintbrushes

With a cup, you can have a tea party with your stuffed animals, store your crayons and brushes, or use it as a gift to a friend. But how do you make a cup without a pottery wheel? You'll use a technique called coil pottery. Are you ready to squish, pat, and roll some clay?

CAUTION: Your finished cup is not food safe. Use for decorative purposes or to pretend play with your toys. To clean, use a damp cloth and wipe clean. Do not submerge in water.

CAUTION: Acrylic paint is not washable. Be sure to protect your art space and wear an apron.

THE STEPS

1. Cover your workspace with two layers of easel paper or Bristol paper. Tape down all the edges.

CONTINUED

CONTINUED

MATERIALS (CONT.)

- ➔ Acrylic paint
- ➔ Paint palette or disposable plate
- ➔ Used toothbrush
- ➔ White glue or decoupage medium

2. Spoon 2 tablespoons of clay and the warm water into a resealable sandwich bag. Seal the bag; then knead and squish the bag until well mixed. This is your slip. The slip will be used as glue. Pour the slip into a small bowl and set it aside.

Helpful Tip: Keep the resealable sandwich bag to pour any leftover slip at the end of the project to use for next time. Slips can be kept in the refrigerator for a week.

3. Roll out a palm-size ball of clay using a rolling pin to about ¼ inch thick, the same thickness of two coins stacked.

4. Cut with a circle cookie cutter. If you're using the bottom of a cup to trace a circle, use a butter knife to cut out the shape.

5. Flip a paper bowl upside down. Place the circle-shaped clay on top. This will help make it easier to work on your cup by lifting it up and allowing you to turn your creation. A paper bowl is best to allow proper drying. Set aside.

Helpful Tip: If you don't have a paper bowl, you can transfer your cup to a sheet of parchment paper when it's time to dry it.

6. Roll out a palm-size ball of clay into a long coil. Use both hands to roll it out as evenly as possible. It's easiest if it's about as thick as your pointer (index) finger. Make the coil as long as you can without getting too thin. Make two or three more coils and set them aside.

7. Score small X marks all around the circle's edge with a toothpick.

8. Spread the slip gently onto the score marks using an ice pop stick. This is called the score-and-slip technique. It's used to attach pieces of clay together.

CONTINUED

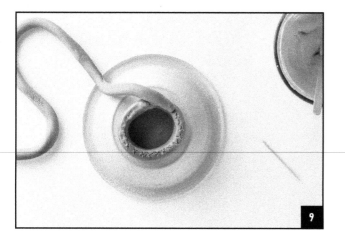

9. Lay one end of a coil onto the score-and-slip area. Gently continue to lay the coil on top of the score and slip. Stop once there is no more score and slip. Cut the coil with a butter knife. Add slip to connect the two ends. With your finger, gently rub to blend the seam of the two ends together.

Helpful Tip: If cutting the coil sounds too tricky, don't worry about it. Leave the coil dangling and continue to the next step.

10. Score and slip the top of your first layer of coil. Continue to score, slip, and lay coil to add more layers until you've reached a height you like. To make a cup to hold crayons, you'll need five to seven layers.

11. Wipe away oozing slip with a clean paintbrush. If there are tiny cracks in your clay, you can dip the paintbrush into the slip and brush it onto the cracks to fill and smooth them out.

12. Dry your work for 7 days to 10 days. You'll know it's still wet if the color of the cup is patchy or if the clay is cold to the touch. Dried clay will be lighter and warmer.

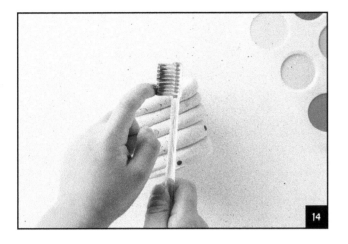

13. Paint a coat (layer) of acrylic paint. Start with the inside of the cup and work your way out. Leave it to dry for 20 minutes. Paint a second coat.

14. Decorate with painted polka dots, hearts, or dashes. To add a speckled effect, dip a used toothbrush into the paint. Brush the tip of your pointer finger across the bristles. The color will spray. Be sure to start slowly to watch the direction of the spray. Aim the spray toward your cup. Leave to dry for 20 minutes.

15. Glaze your cup with white glue. This will seal and protect your cup and give it a matte finish. For a glossy finish, use a glossy decoupage medium.

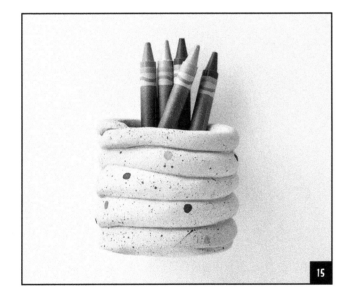

FUN FACT: Not all clays can be air-dried. Most need to be fired in a kiln. When using a technique called reduction firing, the speckled effect occurs naturally when the mineral iron pyrite in the clay melts.

CONTINUED

⬛🅣🅕🅐🅜 CONNECTION: Coil pottery is one of the oldest methods of making cups. One of the newest ways to make a cup is with a 3D printer. Did you know the first 3D object printed was a cup? Have you ever seen a 3D printer in action? Much like our coil cup, the printer coils tiny plastic threads around and around in layers.

NOW TRY THIS!

- ➲ Ready to be challenged? Blend each coiled layer by pressing down the sides with an ice pop stick or your finger. Start with small downward strokes to fill in the lines between each coil. Then blend in further by adding some slip and gently rubbing to smooth out.
- ➲ Have some fun and decorate the top layer of your cup. Bend the last coil to make waves, or why not even braid it?

SCULPT WITH CARDBOARD

TIME: 45 MINUTES

DIFFICULTY LEVEL: CHALLENGING

MEDIUM: ACRYLIC ON CORRUGATED CARDBOARD

TECHNIQUE: LAYERED SCULPTURE

MATERIALS

- Cardboard from a used box
- Pencil
- Ruler
- Scissors
- Template on page 109
- Colored cardstock or construction paper in green
- Hot glue gun and glue sticks
- Acrylic paint in yellow, pink, and red
- Fine-point round paintbrush
- Paint palette or ice cube tray

Did you know you can bend, roll, and layer with cardboard to sculpt it? What if you could also paint, glue, and stick paper bits to it to create a creature like a snail? In this project, we'll learn to work with cardboard!

CAUTION: Hot glue will burn. Do not touch the nozzle of the glue gun or the hot glue until cooled. Younger kids must ask grown-ups to use the hot glue gun. Low-temperature hot glue guns are available for older kids.

CAUTION: Acrylic paint is not washable. Be sure to protect your art space and wear an apron.

CAUTION: Cardboard can be tough to cut, so ask a grown-up to cut the cardboard pieces using sharp scissors or a box knife.

Helpful Tip: Cardboard is made from two flat pieces of paper on the outside and a wavy piece of paper on the inside. The wavy part is called fluting. You can see which way the fluting goes by looking for the bumpy lines. In this project, you'll learn which direction the fluting should be to make it easier to roll and fold. Follow the steps carefully!

CONTINUED

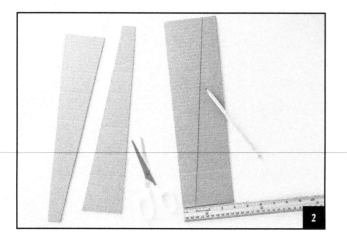

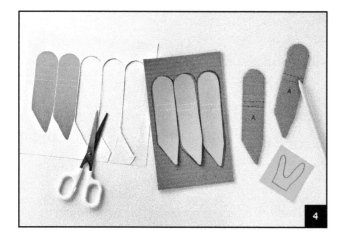

THE STEPS

1. Cut two rectangular pieces of cardboard that measure 4 inches wide × 14 inches tall. The fluting needs to run parallel to the width.

2. On the first piece, measure 1 inch across the bottom and make a small mark. Measure 3 inches across the top and make a small mark. Draw a line between the two marks to create a diagonal line. Repeat for the second piece.

3. Cut along the lines. These pieces will be used for the snail shell. Set them aside.

4. Cut and trace the template on page 109 onto your cardboard to make the snail's body. From tallest to shortest, label them A, B, C, D, and E to keep track. The fluting needs to run parallel to the dashed lines on the template. While you trace, cut, and label the body parts, be sure also to mark where the dashed lines are.

5. Make a total of three pieces for body part A.

6. On colored cardstock, draw and cut out antennas for the snail.

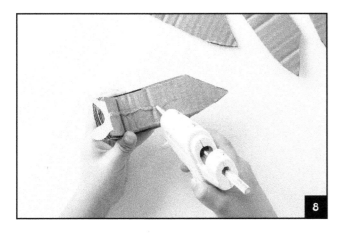

7. Fold along the dashed lines you copied on the cardboard. Layer the body parts from bottom to top in this order: A, A, A, B, C, D, E. Check if the points of the tails line up and match. Doing this is what we call a "dry fit test."

8. After you've tested lining up the body parts, you can hot glue them together. Be careful not to glob on too much glue. The hot glue may squeeze out as you add the layers. Ask a grown-up to help.

9. Next, we'll work on the shell. Match up and layer each strip of the snail's shell made in steps 1 to 3.

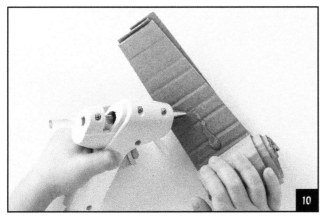

10. You will need a grown-up for this next step. Roll and hot glue the strips starting at the widest end. Roll slowly, bit by bit, adding drops of hot glue between each layer, then wait for the glue to cool before rolling another couple of inches. Continue doing it this way until you reach the end.

11. Hot glue the snail shell to the snail's body.

12. Paint a face on your creation, hot glue the antennas to the snail's head, and curl the antennas.

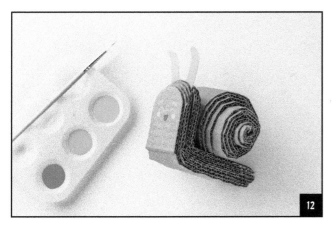

CONTINUED

FUN FACT: In medieval **illuminated manuscripts**, there are doodles of knights in armor ready to attack a snail. One historian once wrote, "Silly knight, it's just a snail!"

Ⓢ**ⓉⒻⒶ**Ⓜ **CONNECTION:** In math, the number phi (ϕ = 1.6180339887498) can be drawn as a geometrical grid that looks a lot like the spiral of a snail's shell. For many years, artists thought this was the **golden ratio** for beauty. Today, photographers still use this grid to help **crop** a photo to create a balanced **composition**.

NOW TRY THIS!

➔ Make the snail shell again, and paint it to see what you can create. A cinnamon bun? A rose? Let the spiral inspire new creations!

➔ Play with layers. Draw circles and glue the layers together. What can you make if you layer 12 circles of the same size? A column? What if the circles were different sizes? Can you make a sphere?

Part III

PUTTING IT ALL TOGETHER

I am proud of you! Look at all the wonderful artwork you've made! Do you realize how much you've learned by doing the projects in this book? You have explored more than twenty-five mediums and discovered more than twenty-two techniques. You have read about art and artists spanning forty-five centuries. You have made mistakes and turned them into works of art. You have explored and shared your emotions and thoughts through art. You have made lines, shapes, and colors while learning a mouthful of new words like *hygroscopic* and *Renaissance*. Most amazing of all, you've made STEAM artworks while having fun doodling, cutting, pasting, sewing, sculpting, and painting.

Now that you've learned so much, what's next? How can you stay an artist, stay inspired, and change the world? Read on to find out.

I'M AN ARTIST!

First, take a minute to congratulate yourself! You made a wall full of art while learning about different mediums and techniques through STEAM. How? Do you remember observing animal patterns and making art with a metaphor for metamorphosis? That was inspired by science. How about technology? Yes, you made a luminary and an e-textile crown! With engineering? Yes again, you sculpted a map of your neighborhood. And math? You measured, balanced, and learned about proportions. Yes, you did *all* that! That's worth celebrating!

Making art with STEAM will help you make art like no one has ever seen before. How? Let's review all the STEAM connections we've made:

STEM inspires art. Artists have made new kinds of art when they were inspired by STEM. In our projects, we learned that Hannah Höch was inspired by the invention of photography to create photomontages and Georges Seurat explored optic science to inspire a new style called pointillism.

STEM is an artist's tool. New discoveries and inventions are being made every day. Using new tools, as we did with our robot to make large scribbles and with our grid to make pixel art, we found new ways to make new kinds of art.

STEM helps us understand our art making. By understanding the science behind our mediums and techniques, as we did with aerial perspective and color mixing, we can explore and experiment with our art-making process.

Art innovates STEM. Art and artists have helped innovate STEM. For example, Eadweard Muybridge discovered how a horse gallops with stop-motion photography. Maria Sibylla Merian debunked the theory of spontaneous generation with her illustrations of metamorphosis. Working across STEAM can bring new truths, ideas, and inspirations.

It's not hard to see how STEAM is all connected. I'm here to cheer you on to make your next STEAM-y work of art!

ART IS ALL AROUND YOU!

How can you get inspired to make art every day? Easy peasy! With your sketchbook, of course! Art is all around you, and an artist will make notes, sketch, ask questions, and doodle. Practice this every day, and you'll end up with 150 sketchbooks, just like the abstract artist, Hilma af Klint. You, too, can be inspired to make unique and new art. Remember when you walked the neighborhood to sketch the shapes of buildings, homes, and cars? Keep doing that. Be inspired by the many shapes, colors, shadows, textures, and patterns around you.

Remember to keep asking questions, like when you asked yourself what a ball of crumpled paper looked like. Ask yourself, "What can I do with an egg carton?" Write down your musings and let these wonderings inspire your art making.

Art is inside you, too. When we ask questions like "What is my favorite color and why?" or "How am I feeling today?" we are looking inside ourselves to inspire our art. Art is a meaningful way to explore who we are. The more you learn about yourself, the more meaning your art will have.

ARTISTS RULE! KEEP CREATING!

You can make art anywhere. You can sculpt castles in the sand, make a bunny appear on a plate of crumbs, and doodle a rainbow on a foggy window. When you leave art behind, you can bring a smile to someone's day. It can make them feel, think, and wonder. Imagine someone had a bad day, and they're sitting at a bus stop worrying about being late. As the bus arrives, they see the rainbow you drew earlier that morning. The person smiles and texts their friend, "I might be a little late, but we can make up the time 🌈." The friend reads this while struggling to finish a science project. When the friend sees the rainbow, it sparks inspiration to build a friendship bridge painted with rainbow colors. One month later, the rainbow bridge wins an award at the science fair. It's incredible how much a little work of art could inspire! Imagine if more kids like you shared art everywhere they went. How fun and beautiful would the world be?

Your learning and art making don't end here. I've left a list of books for you to be inspired by. You can find them in Resources on page 110. Take this list to the library and ask your librarian to help you find them. The journey of an artist never ends. Thank you for letting me come along with you. Keep learning. Keep wondering. Keep making art.

GLOSSARY

ADDITIVE COLOR: A mixing model for light used by scientists and theater light technicians (different from subtractive color, a mixing model for pigments)

AERIAL PERSPECTIVE (OR ATMOSPHERIC PERSPECTIVE): An effect artists use to create depth in their landscape art, giving an illusion of depth, done by playing with a hue's saturation and value

APPROPRIATION: A strategy an artist uses by copying someone else's art and making it slightly different to call it their own art

ART-TO-WEAR (OR WEARABLE ART): A term artists use for handmade art that you can wear

BACKGROUND: The farthest distance in a picture, drawing, or scene

C. (CIRCA): When written before a year, it means "approximately"

COLOR WHEEL: Shaped in a circle, a tool artists use that maps primary, secondary, and tertiary colors

COMPLEMENTARY COLOR: A color that is opposite to another on the color wheel and makes a shade of gray when mixed

COMPOSITION: How color, line, shape, texture, form, and shape are positioned, placed, or organized in an artwork

CONTOUR: The outside shape of a form

CREATIVE PROCESS: The steps to take to make art

CROP: How an artist decides to cut off or frame the edges of a photo, drawing, or painting

CUBIST: An artist that made art during the cubism art movement in Paris between 1907 and 1914 that often had a shattered-cube look to the art

DADA (OR DADAISM): An art movement between 1916 and 1924 and well known to be "anti-art" at the time

DEPTH: The distance away from you

FOREGROUND: The part of a painting, photo, drawing, or scene that is closest to the viewer

FORM: The whole shape of anything that takes up a three-dimensional space

FOUND OBJECTS (OR FOUND ART): A term artists use for art that is made from something they've found

GOLDEN RATIO: A grid that resembles a snail shell that artists use to help with their composition

ILLUMINATED MANUSCRIPTS: A handwritten book with painted pictures and decorated in gold, made between the years 400 and 1600 CE

IMPRESSIONIST: Artists during the impressionism art movement between about 1867 and 1886, where artists focused on painting light

LANDSCAPE: Artworks of land, like painted mountains, valleys, or fields

MASTERPIECE: The greatest and best work of art

MEDIUM: The material or the type of art; for example, paint, canvas, pencil, and so on.

METAPHOR: Comparing two things that aren't normally related

MIXED MEDIA: A term artists use when they use many mediums together in one artwork

MODERN ART: A nontraditional movement in art from the 1860s to the 1970s

MURAL: Art that's made on a wall

MUSING: A term artists use for their thoughts, usually related to inspiration

NEGATIVE SPACE: The empty or "white" space around or in a work of art

PAPIER-MÂCHÉ: Translates to "chewed paper" and is a method of using pieces of paper and paste to make a sculpture

PHOTOMONTAGE: A collage using photographs

PIXELS: Tiny squares that make an image appear on a digital screen

POINTILLISM: A painting technique or style using many tiny colored dots of paint to make an image

POSITIVE SPACE: The filled space of the art

PRIMARY COLORS: The colors of red, yellow, and blue (RYB) on a color wheel for paints; or the colors red, green, and blue (RGB) for light; or the colors cyan, magenta, and yellow (CMY) for printing

PRINTMAKING: Artworks made for copying, like a stamp

PROCESS ART: A technique that focuses on enjoying how the art is made without an idea or plan of how it will turn out

PROPORTION: The size of something and how it relates to a whole; for example, a face drawn bigger than the body has a cartoonlike proportion

RENAISSANCE ART: An art movement in Europe that focused on classical art and techniques, made from c. 1350 to 1620 CE

RHYTHM: When art has an element, like line or color, that repeats

SCIENTIFIC ILLUSTRATION (BIOLOGICAL ILLUSTRATION): A drawing that shows information to a scientist, like the parts of a bug or the different sections of the brain

SECONDARY COLOR: Colors that appear when you mix two primary colors in equal amounts

STILL LIFE: A term artists use for artwork that shows only objects sitting on a table or shelf

STOP-MOTION PICTURE: A series of images that are shown one at a time superfast to make it look like they're moving

SUBTRACTIVE COLOR: A mixing model for pigment, like paint or markers, used by artists

TECHNIQUE: The way an art medium is used

TERTIARY COLOR: The color that appears when you mix a primary color with a secondary color in equal amounts

VISUAL MERCHANDISER: A person who works at a store to display products

GRID PAPER FOR EXPRESS IT
WITH PIXELS (PAGE 59)

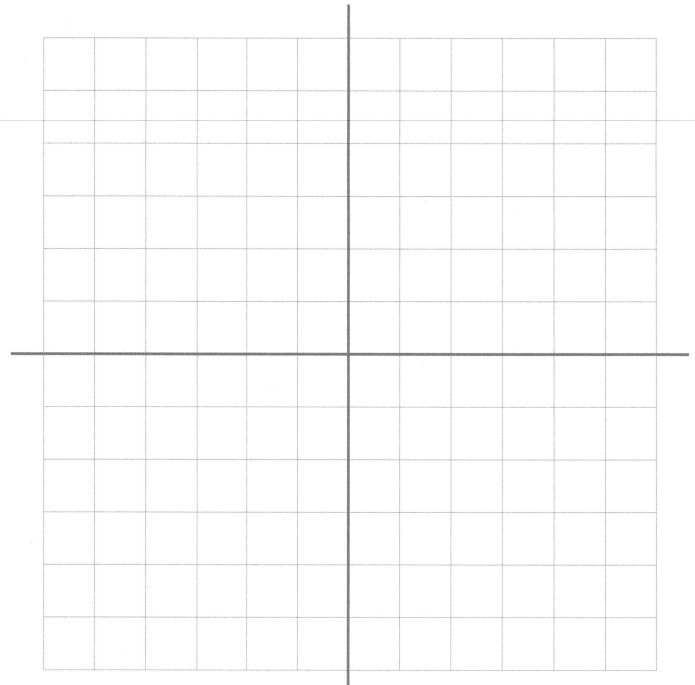

TEMPLATE FOR SCULPT
WITH CARDBOARD (PAGE 95)

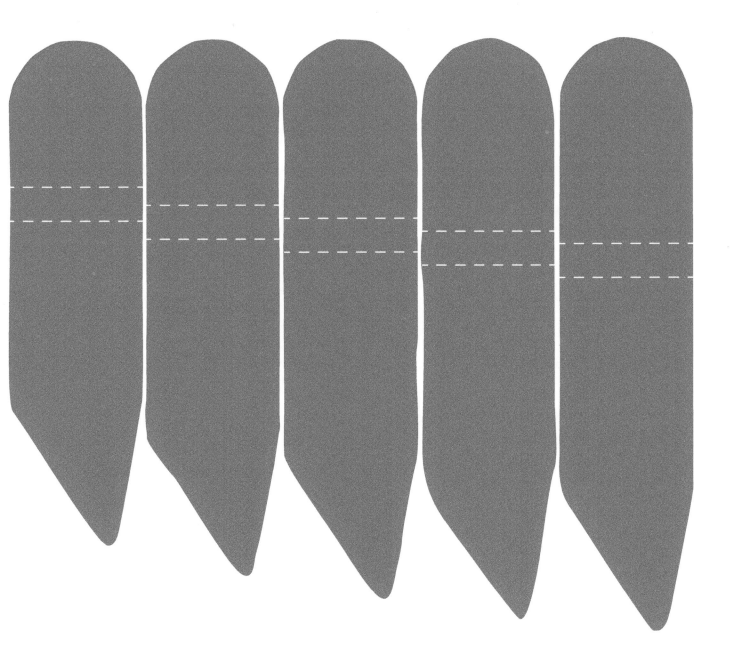

RESOURCES

STORYBOOKS TO INSPIRE STEAM PROJECTS

How can STEM inspire art or art inspire STEM? Read these books to inspire you to make STEAM.

Boxitects
by Kim Smith

Georgia's Terrific, Colorific Experiment
by Zoe Persico

The Girl Who Drew Butterflies: How Maria Merian's Art Changed Science
by Joyce Sidman

The Girl Who Thought in Pictures: The Story of Dr. Temple Grandin
by Julia Finley Mosca, illustrated by Daniel Rieley

How to Code a Sandcastle
by Josh Funk, illustrated by Sara Palacios

STORYBOOKS TO INSPIRE ART MAKING

Feeling stuck or frustrated? Read these books to inspire you make mistakes and move past creative blocks.

Arlo Draws an Octopus
by Lori Mortensen, illustrated by Rob Sayegh Jr.

Be a Maker
by Katey Howes, illustrated by Elizabet Vuković

Beautiful Oops!
by Barney Saltzberg

The Dot
by Peter H. Reynolds

Hey, Wall: A Story of Art and Community
by Susan Verde, illustrated by John Parra

Many Shapes of Clay: A Story of Healing
by Kenesha Sneed

Maybe Something Beautiful: How Art Transformed a Neighborhood
by F. Isabel Campoy and Theresa Howell, Illustrated by Rafael López

Parker Looks Up: An Extraordinary Moment
by Parker Curry and Jessica Curry, illustrated
by Brittany Jackson

The Perfect Square
by Michael Hall

BOOKS ABOUT ARTISTS

Read these books to learn the many
journeys of an artist and how they've
been inspired.
The Bug Girl: Maria Merian's Scientific Vision
by Sarah Glenn Marsh, illustrated by
Filippo Vanzo

Frida Kahlo and Her Animalitos
by Monica Brown, illustrated by John Parra

Henri's Scissors
by Jeanette Winter

*A History of Pictures for Children: From Cave
Paintings to Computer Drawings*
by David Hockney and Martin Gayford, illustrated by Rose Blake

Jean-Michel Basquiat
by Maria Isabel Sánchez Vegara, illustrated by
Luciano Lozano

Picasso's Trousers
by Nicholas Allan

*Sewing Stories: Harriet Powers' Journey from
Slave to Artist*
by Barbara Herkert, illustrated by
Vanessa Brantley-Newton

Sonia Delaunay, A Life of Color
by Cara Manes, illustrated by Fatinha Ramos

Women Artists A to Z
by Melanie LaBarge, illustrated by
Caroline Corrigan

Yayoi Kusama: From Here to Infinity
by Sarah Suzuki, illustrated by Ellen Weinstein

THE ART AND ARTISTS MENTIONED IN THIS BOOK

Visit these websites with a grown-up to
learn more about some of the art and artists
mentioned in this book.
Ai-Da
Ai-DaRobot.com

Clara Peeters
Collections.LACMA.org/node/209186

Differantly (DFT)
DFT.art

Eadweard Muybridge
KingstonHeritage.org.uk/muybridge

Georges Seurat
Guggenheim.org/artwork/artist/georges-seurat

Hannah Höch
MoMA.org/artists/2675

Hilma of Klint
HilmaAfKlint.se

Jaune Quick-to-See Smith
JauneQuicktoSeeSmith.org

Jean-Michel Basquiat
Basquiat.com

Judith Scott
CreativeGrowth.org/judith-scott

Leonardo da Vinci, *Mona Lisa*
Focus.Louvre.fr/en/mona-lisa

Leonardo da Vinci, *The Vitruvian Man*
GallerieAccademia.it/en/node/1582

Marcel Duchamp, *Bicycle Wheel*
MoMA.org/collection/works/81631

Maria Sibylla Merian
BotanicalArtAndArtists.com/about-maria
-sibylla-merian.html

Michelangelo Pistoletto
Pistoletto.it

Pablo Picasso
NGA.gov/collection/artist-info.1783.html

Poul Henningsen
MoMA.org/collection/works/3215

Salvador Dalí, *The Persistence of Time*
MoMA.org/collection/works/79018

Shepard Fairey
ObeyGiant.com

Shigetaka Kurita
MoMA.org/collection/works/196070

Wassily Kandinsky
ArtsandCulture.Google.com/story/the
-sound-of-colors/OALymHuhPl1jLg

Yayoi Kusama
Yayoi-Kusama.jp

STEAM PROJECTS AND ACTIVITIES

Check out these links and books for activities and lessons to dive deeper into STEAM.
Khan Academy, Imagineering in a Box Course
KhanAcademy.org/humanities/hass
-storytelling/imagineering-in-a-box

Institute for Arts Integration and STEAM,
Free Lesson Plans
ArtsIntegration.com/topics/curriculum
/free-lesson-plans

Leonardo's Art Workshop: Invent, Create, and Make STEAM Projects Like a Genius
by Amy Leidtke

Math Art + Drawing Games for Kids
by Karyn Tripp

The School of Art: Learn How to Make Great Art with 40 Simple Lessons
by Teal Triggs

INDEX

ACKNOWLEDGMENTS

A warm thank-you goes to the team at Rockridge Press for putting this book together, inviting me to write, and giving me a space to release my creative energy. Thank you to Eliza Kirby, the amazing editor of this book. Thank you to my family and friends who checked in, supported, and nudged me to keep going. Thank you to my brother for the much-needed lighting direction. Thank you to my husband for contributing the left side of your brain and for everything you do for our family. Thank you most of all to my little one, who, at age five, helped test the projects, shared opinions, and lent two little hands.

ABOUT THE AUTHOR

 **Lucy Song** was a curious child, often found "borrowing" books and materials from an arts and crafts shop in the basement of her childhood home. She spent her time reading, making, and tinkering, unknowingly shaping her skills to become the youngest creative director for fashion retailer Le Château Inc. When Lucy became a mom, she noticed how little the inequities in early education have changed since her childhood. Feeling sad and angry, she spent four days and nights writing her debut self-published e-book, *Raising Little Allies-to-Be*. Upon release, it hit over 30,000 downloads in its first week. Lucy continues to work to empower young, curious, and creative minds as an author, as an adjunct professor of art and design at Seneca College, and by sharing her artful changemaking resources at WithWonder.co.